THE ENCHANT

ROBIN FEDDEN was brought up largely in France. He worked for many years for the National Trust, and travelled extensively in the Middle East. Apart from his love of travel he was also an enthusiastic walker and mountaineer.

THE
ENCHANTED
MOUNTAINS

A Quest in the Pyrenees

ROBIN
FEDDEN

Foreword by Nicholas Crane

JOHN MURRAY
Albemarle Street, London

Some of the author's other books

Crusader Castles
Syria & Lebanon
Alpine Ski-tour
The Land of Egypt

Ma tu, perchè ritorni a tanta noia?
perchè non sali il dilettoso monte,
ch'è principio e cagion di tutta gioia?
DANTE: *Inferno* I

First published in 1962
by John Murray (Publishers) Ltd,
50 Albemarle Street, London W1S 4BD

This paperback edition 2002

A catalogue record for this book is available from the British Library

ISBN 0-7195-5523-X

Printed and bound in Great Britain by
Bookmarque Ltd, Croydon, Surrey

CONTENTS

*Notes on the Spanish Pyrenees from the
Val d'Estos to the Noguera Pallaresa*

INDEX

FOREWORD

A few years ago I took a walk along the ranges that rise and fall across Europe from Finisterre to Istanbul. The Pyrenees proved an intoxicating prelude; a curtain of stone and ice draped between the plains of Spain and France. By the time I had tramped erratically to the Enchanted Mountains, I was bewitched, but it wasn't until I'd read this book that I fully understood why.

Forty years have passed since Robin Fedden unrolled his swansdown sleeping-bag beneath the 'dome of the sky', a blink in geological time but an age in the passing of human geography. No longer is it possible (sadly) to stumble into bear traps or to gaze at night's ceiling without catching the wink of satellite or jetliner. But the greater part of this upland wilderness remains intact. Troupes of horned izards still stalk the Fourcanade, and Maledetta – the Accursed Mountain – keeps the last of its glacier 'tied like a napkin round its neck'. And a new generation of Don Miguels lodge easily on rough-hewn bars, ready with advice on false cols and tracks which beguile and yet lead nowhere.

With his soft-footed erudition and sensitive insights, Robin Fedden effortlessly lifts the contours from his text, turning a cornice of snow into a Hokusai wave, a panorama into an off-print of Patinir. Rare is the writer who can celebrate the *roche moutonée* as eloquently as *Liliastrum Bertolina*. Apart from tragic Don Miguel, the author's Pyrenean guides were Packe and Russell, Spender and Belloc, the quartet of pioneers whose spirits still march through these misted peaks. Robin Fedden is up there with them.

Nicholas Crane

PREFACE

This book is not primarily about mountaineering. It is an account of satisfactions to be found in a little-visited region of the Spanish Pyrenees. For the sake of the story I have combined three journeys my wife and I made between 1953 and 1957, and I have taken my liberties with the sequence of events. In the same interest, I have said little of those who were with us at one time or another. Yet their company and friendship savour three Pyrenean summers.

R. F.

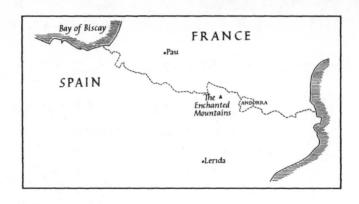

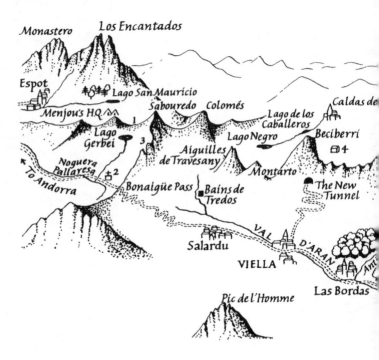

1 Cresta d'Amitjes   2 Nuestra Senhora de los Are

Aerial perspective of the area of the
ENCHANTED MOUNTAINS
in the Central Pyrenees

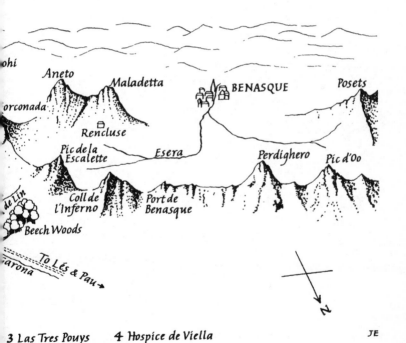

ohi

Aneto

Maladetta

BENASQUE

Posets

orconada

Rencluse

Pic de la Escalette

Esera

Perdighero

Pic d'Oo

de Lin

Coll de l'Inferno

Port de Benasque

Beech Woods

To Lés & Pau →

arona

N

3 Las Tres Pouys   4 Hospice de Viella   JE

I

THE LURE

There was no wind. The mist moved tentatively, groping its way up the mountain. We first felt its touch not far above tree-level, and a moment later were enveloped. The early sun went out. With it went the ranged peaks and the depths of air over the Gave de Pau. We became, the two of us, shadowy figures, 'men as trees walking'; we stumbled among the dwarf juniper as though stricken with Meunier's Disease.

In mist one draws closer to the anchoring ground at one's feet. This, the single thing visible, grows more real. Its scale changes. Now grass blades shining with moisture became giant fronds; in buds and shoots we saw green crockets and finials, vegetable gargoyles spouting dew; pebbles gleamed with the brilliance of precious stones; enormous ants with rounded personalities moved on expeditions through complex country. At each step we destroyed cats' cradles of cobweb and devastated the intricate landscape of beetles. All this had been unnoticed in a wider air.

We were soon lost. A compass is reliable until needed. In the lapping mist there followed consultation and difference of opinion. Casting about the steepening slopes, we struck by chance the grassy col where the north-west ridge of the Pic d'Astazaou abuts. We had lost a couple of hours.

About us the grey lace was warm, almost lascivious in its touch, yet there was danger in its very gentleness. We hesitated, but not for long. The clean rock-rib fitted snugly into the turf, like the arm of a well-upholstered chair, and was by repute one of the best-sustained in the Pyrenees.

The climb that followed was never of itself difficult. The difficulty and strangeness derived from the warm bandage on our eyes. Sometimes the mist, for no obvious reason, would vibrate as though we stood at the throbbing head of a sound conductor. We suffered the shattering blare of horns in Gavarnie as motor coaches forced their way up the village street five thousand feet below; we heard a saddled donkey braying as it waited for tourists outside the Hôtel des Voyageurs; we endured the roar of a distant waterfall. These sounds were cut off arbitrarily, leaving us alone in our grey cocoon.

We climbed sightless and bemused, our doubts and certainties equally at fault. If a puff of air momentarily lifted the mist's hem it was to tease and dizzy us with unfamiliar sense of space. Neighbouring buttresses and towers bore down like ships towards us, only to disappear. When at last a brusque gust tore a whole curtain aside to reveal precipices, green meadows, and toy houses, I realized how much still stretched above. The reflex glance at my watch told that we were climbing too slowly. Time like distance had seemed not to exist until the wider perspective, the briefly lifting mist, showed, in two senses, where we stood. In the mountains such revelations are apt to come in time. It is in the confidence bred at lower levels that one sees too late which white hand proffers the poisoned martini, which croquet lawn, diapered with shade, is an operating table.

Mist, time, and our apprehension, were now against us. In the shifting element even our rock-rib seemed unstable, and mere balance an achievement. My eyes monstrously deluded me, as they will do looking into water. There was the same refraction and I reached for footholds where none were. Through the deceiving blanket we groped steadily up. Below me the rope disappeared in the mist like a hawser into deep water and gave no sense of security. R. would emerge beside me like a swimmer surfacing, the grey spray dripping from her. There came a moment, as I tired, when it seemed almost better to rot where we clung than raise another hand or foot. Two vultures, with mangy yellow necks and piebald wings, slid past and stared. Such birds at such times seem portents.

Our undertaking appeared endless and beyond reasonable effort. Then the angle of the rock eased, and a moment later we were dazedly on the summit. A mountain top when one can see nothing offers little reassurance. True, we could sit on the shattered rocks, and we could eat; but it was late, we were blind, and the comfortable valley lay thousands of feet below. There was small chance of striking the route down the glacier and across the polished slabs. Then, as dubious we munched our garlic sausage, the desired, the miraculous happened. There was a motion, a slow retraction, prompted by some obscure barometric change, and the mists, serpent-like, began to uncoil from the depths. Wreathing upward, they passed in long convolutions. The summit grew lighter. The moment came—

it was sudden—when we were clear shapes and no longer isolated from the rest of the world. Below us were baths of air and the articulation of landscape. Above our heads the medium which had taxed us and dramatized our day was melting and vanishing. Soon it had gone. The hesitating judgements, the faltering technique, seemed to have had no real basis.

With a sense of deliverance we strolled across bright snow and dropped down a band of rock to the glacier. The mountain had neither defeated nor imprisoned us. Each step was joy. Our eyes, long starved of distance, were free of wide views and drank the afternoon light. At the first green alp we halted. There, sprawled among wild iris whose deep colour burned like cold metal, we were rewarded with that sense of a participating landscape, of a partnership with the mountains, that is so satisfying and no doubt so baseless. The day seemed to have been not wholly our own affair.

Time passed. The sun's rays streamed almost level over France, and the peaks collected troughs of shadow at their feet. In the long valley eastward the light grew honey-coloured, dense as liquid. It was our last day and we recalled the summer's pleasure; drinking Jurançon with *truite aux amandes* on a hot night in a bower of oleanders; looking into the tops of flowering trees from the cloister at St Bertrand de Comminges; the creaking boards and the smell of a snoring inn at Gabas whence we crept before dawn, carrying our boots; the floury new snow on the summit of the Pic du Midi and the parched slopes below dotted with sheep droppings: izard *en casserole* and the affronted glance of a huge buck surprised on the Balaitous ridge; the rotten rock of the Arriel and the solid Pic du Pallas; the cold on the Petit Vignemale that made my fingers white and clumsy as tallow candles; a green view of alps and byres, precisely defined, two thousand feet beneath a curving snow slope; and every day, drifts of *ranunculus pyrenaeus*. We also remembered the little French couple. On their free Saturday they had walked from Lourdes, at midnight had bivouacked briefly under a rock and had then climbed the north face of the Pique-Longue. We met them late on Sunday setting out for the valley, a five-hour descent. In the comfort of a mountain hut, we marvelled at this dedication, to marvel further at the girl's reply, 'Il faut savoir souffrir pour la montagne.'

Easy among the irises, we contemplated the weeks. They were still with us, but we knew that tomorrow as we started north by motor they would have become the past. One thing we did not know: how much of the future, of further summers, the day still obscurely held.

The Hôtel du Cirque is the last building, the highest point of habitation, to which tourists penetrate on foot and donkey to wonder, very rightly, at the Cirque de Gavarnie. At sunset the noisy tide retreats; the hotel is left alone below the precipices. The bar was empty when we returned; the only trace of the day's indignities were the stubs, papers and ice-cream cartons beneath the marble-topped tables. A big girl with sunburnt arms but strangely white bosom had sprinkled water on the wooden floor and was sweeping. Soon all would be decent again.

We dropped our ropes and rucksacks; relieved of their weight we felt lightfooted, six inches taller, and recognized another reward that comes at the end of such a day.

Someone has said that mountains offer only two pleasurable moments, of which the second is the more intense: arrival on the summit, and safe return to hut or inn. Even a disillusioned mountaineer would surely add a third: the moment when a drink is set beside him on a table. The reassuring thud as a full carafe is slapped on the wooden trestle in an alpine hut, the rich note of glasses on café marble or their singing contact with a green-painted iron table in the sun: these are part of the music of the hills. The third moment of the day was now ours: a long moment, for not less than three drinks allow one to savour return, to review the triumphs of the day, and if necessary to explain its failures. Behind the bar Monsieur Vergez, as befitted a competent inn-keeper and an old guide, showed appropriate interest in our expedition as he poured the drinks. The glasses approached; there was a chink of ice, and we watched, that familiar visual pleasure, the liquid clouding as water was added to the anis. It was a still evening. Through the open window we heard the glacier stream slapping on the rocks as it swirled to Gavarnie. Darkness gathered in the corners of the room, seeping in from the huge drifts that piled under the rock faces of the Cirque. With our second drink Monsieur Vergez switched on the light. The yellowish bulb pulsed unevenly, like the palpitation of an ageing heart.

The man who entered acknowledged Monsieur Vergez's greeting with a half-lifted hand. As he looked slowly round the room, our presence seemed to evoke a faint expression of distaste. Leaning on the zinc, he spoke in whispers, yet without urgency, as one might talk who had temporarily lost his voice. A cigarette smouldered at his lower lip. Not at first sight a pleasing man: a sallow complexion; a mouth faintly stained at one corner with tobacco smoke; a long nose, the nostrils thin as the gills of a fish; and inky hair growing far back from a receding forehead. Further the whole head was inadequately supported, for his dirty black suit appeared to have no defined shape, to be subject to no internal pressures. The head, the feet in pointed mud-bespattered shoes, and the lazy yellow hands, emerged from the black serge as surprisingly as do the extremities of a tortoise.

His confidential business reminded me that traffic still sometimes passed at night, and better so, over the mule tracks of the central Pyrenees. Monsieur Vergez shook his head. If the stranger was disappointed, he did not show it. The whispering ended, and we heard his Spanish accent. With a tired movement, he indicated our table. We caught our names in the murmur of their now desultory conversation. Gradually silence fell on the bar. Our host went to see about dinner. The torpor which made it difficult for the stranger to take the cigarette from his lips invaded him utterly. Propped against the bar, he was motionless, eyes glazed but unblinking. To participate so little in one's surroundings must, I thought, call for unusual lethargy or detachment.

He seemed to be with us not at all, when I heard his voice:

'What sort of mountains are these?' he said without expression. 'And this, what sort of country?' As if to look at it, he turned his head (slowly, as some iguana might turn) towards the open window. We turned too. It was now dark outside; one could see nothing. 'And what of all these people?'

'Oh, we rather like this area,' I answered.

'Because, with my respect'—the nostrils flickered—'you are ignorant of what lies beyond, eastward.'

'That's true.'

'A pity. Those valleys and mountains are unvisited, the trout in the lakes are as big as dogs, in summer the lowest snows lie a long day by mule from the highroad. Our eagles'—he must have meant the lammergeier—'carry off children. Brandy also is very cheap. . . .' Here he smiled wanly, and it was most surprising.

'You have never heard'—it was merely wry reflection—'of the Gran Tuc de Colomés, of the Gran Peguera, of the Montarto and the Sabouredo, of the Black Lake, or the Baths of Tredos? Probably never even heard—' he expelled the dying stub from his lips and drew a fresh cigarette from his pocket—'never even heard of Los Encantados: the naked twins with the Lake of San Mauricio at their feet. Best of all are the Encantados, the rocks smooth as steel.'

There was an urgent tap on the terrace door. The stranger slowly drained his glass. 'They all know me in the Val d'Aran and beyond. If you come ask for Don Miguel.'

He crossed the room deliberately as he had entered. 'Of course, I have never climbed the Encantados: I only walk on business.'

The door closed, leaving us with the dog-trout, the roc-like eagles, the deserted peaks and valleys, above all with the Enchanted Mountains. We took them in, as it were, to our dinner. I suspected they might be with us for a long time.

*   *   *

Los Encantados, Els Encantats, Montagnes enchantées: the names, varying with the maps, Spanish, Catalan, and French, deprived them of definition. Their position was also indefinite, for again the maps did not agree. That they placed them in a lacustrine region was added mystery; lakes seemed unnatural above the dry foothills of Aragon. Studying a map is like getting to know a face, but these differing sheets did not bring the features into focus. The Enchanted Mountains had no clear outline. Imagination supplied it; so their compulsion grew.

Books told no more than maps. Count Russell (of whom more later) knew nothing of the Encantados; the systematic Packe did not visit them; nor Harold Spender. Even Belloc, quartering the Pyrenees with staff, blanket, and *alpagates*, spoke of them only by hearsay as 'exceedingly rugged and tangled . . . a wilderness of rocky peaks and lakes'. But a winter's reading filled in the foreground. We came to know through others, mainly dead, peaks we were to climb in our approach to the Encantados. We were later able to recognize the Trou du Toro where the waters of the Aneto plunge to the underworld, Mahomet's

Bridge, the Accursed Col, and the pass of the Silver Spring.

The expert, who lives in Toulouse, wrote to me about the birds and the animals and told of the Malta fever in shepherd huts, but of the Encantados spoke obliquely. I liked his old-fashioned prose. 'Vous allez parcourir', he wrote, 'une région particulièrement pauvre et déshéritée: il n'y a pas un seul refuge gardé. Vous ne trouverez que des *orris*, cabanes de bergers à demi-souterraines, recouvertes de bouse de vache et infestées de vermine. C'est un séjour peu favorable à des personnes qui pratiquent une hygiène minutieuse. . . . En dehors d'un soricidé, de l'isard, et de l'ours, dont la rencontre est peu souhaitable, la faune pyrénéenne des vertébrés n'offre aucune particularité.' The last point was fortunate since the only relevant fauna ran to ten volumes and was out of print. Further it was clear that I should rarely have a mule to carry a library. 'Il est impossible', he wrote, 'de parcourir les régions faîtières des Pyrénées en compagnie d'une mule ou de tout autre solipède.' *Solipède?* The *Grande Encyclopédie* knew nothing of it, but I envisaged a philosophic creature, one-legged, something between a stork and a Dinka. It would have been enjoyable to travel in such company. As generous as his prose, the expert sent me the *Guide Soubiron*. The author had died many years earlier, but no one had threaded the Pyrenees more exhaustively. Forty peregrinations were credited to Professor Soubiron, and a peak honoured his name, but the only mention of the Encantados was a tantalizing footnote in which I detected the faintest disapproval, a mere reference to a party which in 1926 had effected in the region 'de nombreuses premières on prati-quant l'alpinisme acrobatique'. The less I learnt of the Encantados the larger they loomed.

*　　　　*　　　　*

Leading south-west across France, the fast roads end where you twist into the Limousin, not far from the last slate-roofed village and the first oxen. The splashes of shadow across N 21 alter their shape, for they are now laid by acacia trees. The detail of the landscape becomes more carefully worked, more idiosyncratic. Even the boulders on the barren *causses* have personality. Murderous shrikes balance on the telephone wires. There are hedges of honey-suckle and fields of lavender, improbable on a waterless astringent soil. Only when you descend to the plain of the Garonne, perhaps above a field of blue flax, near Pamiers or Auch, are the Pyrenees suddenly there, the white summits strung out remote but clear. They are not land-scape; for these things in the sky have no link with the vineyards, the asphalt road, the red soil of Béarn or Roussillon. They do not even relate to the horizon, for haze obscures the foothills. The snows float disembodied above a shimmering heat that makes them tremble like lilies resting on water. The cool apparitions in the sky amaze, and the motor creeps over a dusty crumbling plain.

Between this first revelation and any point where roads climb purposefully into the mountains lies the foothill country, the country obscured by a blue haze. Like the Pyrenees themselves, the region is little frequented by those who travel today. It was once otherwise. Yet deserted by

21

fashion, Pau has acquired a poetry it never knew when the English club was exclusive, when persons of taste extolled the view from the Boulevard des Pyrénées, and when the sycophantic *Guide Bleu* found the splendours of its sixteenth-century court revived in the winter 'Season'. The enormous villas were once fresh painted, and the palms in the gardens were trim and beardless. Carried on the westerly breeze, the baying of foxhounds in those days floated over the Gave de Pau from the heights beyond Aubertin. The well-born, the well-provided, and the scheming, manœuvred for power and position in this belt of country. Short, yet imposing in his homburg, the English King sometimes graced the manœuvres. The disposition of the forces in these green foothills, the grand strategy, the tactics, the bold social sorties, the bankruptcies and marriages, were noted in a dozen capitals. The conflict cannot have been less ruthless in the Béarn, the values which touched off the powder less meretricious, than they are elsewhere, but forgotten battlefields acquire charm. Salons achieve dignity when those who frequented them are dead. They acquire 'the poetry of the thing outlived . . . telling so of connexions but tasting so of differences'. The ghosts of pleasure are more real than those who pursue it, and the monuments left in these foothills fifty and a hundred years ago are compelling: the pump rooms with their palmaria, the gilded *Salles de Jeux*, the shady promenades, the tea-rooms, and the shuttered peeling villas. All now outmoded. To drive up the Boulevard du Casino at Bagnères de Bigoree in a creaking horse-drawn carriage, to pass the thermal springs ('sources sulfates de calciques à minéralisation relativement forte'), and to halt at the Grand Hotel Victoria is to be beset by phantoms. No forgotten watering places are in their way more populous than these of the abandoned Pyrenean *préalpes*.

The quiet hotel in the Place Gramont at Pau is furnished in the Biedermeyer style. One may enjoy the pleasure of walking ten full paces to an ample bath with lion-paw feet. In our bedroom, almost a year after we had left the Hôtel du Cirque above Gavarnie, R. spread and checked our gear, incongruous amid mahogany veneer: ropes and axes, sleeping-bags, boots, and deceptive Spanish maps. Later we stood at sunset on the Boulevard des Pyrénées, watching the distant range draw nearer. The limpid evening sky clarified its outline; it seemed to rise, almost to impend, above the darkening woods and fields. As though a burning iron were for a moment laid on the snow, the highest summits flared red. It was an effect that the ghosts who watched with us had been accustomed to speak of. Next day, a day in mid-June, at the Pont d'Espagne we crossed, where the ghosts had rarely ventured, by the Val d'Aran into the province of Lerida.

*　　　*　　　*

The passport and customs officials are established at Lès, a mile or two beyond the frontier. The village street was hung with coloured streamers and its electric bulbs were tricked out with paper collars like cutlets, but all was silent in the early afternoon. As if sleeping sickness had stricken the village a body was crumpled over a café table and two more slumped in the shade of a wall. Doors stood wide open. The inhabitants, overwhelmed by sleep, had stumbled to their beds without a thought. One sensed the dead weight of bodies on mattresses, on couches, even overcome in lavatories, deep, deep in sleep. Not one turned or cried out in a dream. They were engulfed. The intake of breath and its fluttering expiration from hundreds of lips was the only motion in the village. We halted at the customs barrier, oddly set between taverns and shops, and there we waited. When at last I blew the horn, the noise rebounded from the walls. The man who emerged from the shuttered office into the hot sun seemed in pain. Laying a finger on his lips, he muttered thickly, 'St John, the Feast of St John. Nothing until five.' It was the aftermath of the saint's enormous bacchanal, the long restorative sleep. I recognized the acrid smell of wine, and sniffing found the still street full of it. Like an invisible haze it hung heavier than air. What a night we had missed.

We escaped to the river. Here was a whisp of breeze and a delicious sense of cold for the torrent was still large with melted snow. We hung over the bridge and watched a trout in clear water below a boulder; just free of the tugging current, it seemed asleep like the drugged village. A clock struck the quarters. Shadows began to fill gullies on the hillside that rose steeply behind the church. Still they slept. There was an inn by the bridge and through the open door we could see in a dark room the glint that meant glasses and bottles. Passing from the brightness and the companionable talk of the river, we found the room obscure and silent. Not immediately did we make out the black figure lodged easily against the bar, someone awake and almost upright. It was Don Miguel. He held a glass, and above his head flies scudded in erratic orbits. He eyed us distantly as from a perch and I expected his lids to close upwards as do the eyelids of birds; yet he recognized us. 'So you have taken my advice,' he said, and then, surprisingly, 'I am glad you have come.' The innkeeper emerged yawning, running his hands through his tousled hair, still dazed as though returned from a long journey. He buttoned his shirt and poured us a manzanilla.

The waking of Lès that evening was like the Resurrection. Stretching their arms above their heads, they rose from bed and bench and roadside, moving shakily at first but with guarded elation as they found their pain abated. The throbbing temples and the parched lips, the agony of the morning, had been shed in sleep. In air grown cool, they smiled to themselves at the miracle, and from doorsteps greeted each other as though a new life had begun. Drifting up the street (treading quietly for they still felt the fragility of their new state), or grouped in talk on the bridge, they had the serene and aimless air of the Redeemed in early paintings.

The inn terrace overhung the river, and with drinks and erring maps upon a table we listened to Don Miguel. He told us of hidden valleys, of small landmarks to be engraved on the mind, of overhangs easily turned by ledges known to shepherds, of false cols, of beguiling tracks that led nowhere, and of Aragon seen golden from remote snow summits. He even lingered fondly over the description of scree and bog. When the lights in their paper frills were switched on and the strung garlands swelled with colour, the hills around and the river at our feet retreated into darkness. Though we could now see the water only where it foamed against a rock or tore over a shallow, it provided the unbroken murmur against which Don Miguel's precise instructions were set. I did not then realize that these instructions, accurate in every particular, were mainly acquired at second hand or suspect the tragic nature of his eunuch love for the mountains.

Voice and water hypnotized us. Before we went to bed, our route had been diverted to the Pic d'Aneto. The highest summit of the Pyrenees was to be a preface to the Encantados. We were obscurely glad of the diversion, and it was the first of many side turnings that we took. Simply enough we could have gone straight for our goal, but perhaps it had grown too important for a cavalier approach. Like any mountain which comes to mean much, it had ceased to be solely a technical problem. We seemed already to have an understanding with the Encantados, and if we climbed them it would not be only on our feet. Like a love affair that is inevitable, our meeting could take its time. We could afford to wait and in so doing increase the splendour of the Encantados and their stature. Delay was respect. Perhaps also it hinted a fear that these mountains were not all I had, even at this early stage, imagined. For their sake and ours, it was important that the approach should be circumspect.

When we left early next morning, and Don Miguel with us, Lès again was silent but enjoying a lighter sleep. As we drove up the Val d'Aran, the pastures looked lifeless, tripe-grey in the half-light. Vapour from the river obscured the stars. The road was pot-holed, and the air cold. Anticipation and unfamiliarity alone made the dark start exciting. Don Miguel was bound for his own Salardu, the village at the head of the valley, and we dropped him at the bridge where one turns aside to Las Bordas. He had strangely impressed us and we received his last advice almost with reverence. As he moved up the whitening road, I knew as one knows without seeing, that his walk, over-poised, over-slow, concealed a limp. We later discovered that as a boy he had been trampled herding cattle on the Pleta de Los Gavachos. The accident unfitted him for the mountains, yet left him with a mountain passion, a thing rarely felt by those born among them. By robbing him of his occupation it had also launched him on dubious business ironically linked with passes he would never cross. The reason for his insistent, precise instructions became clear, and later even clearer. We were his envoys, and our achievements and mistakes would be his. As we crossed the bridge, I wondered what limp drove me from human beings to places not always comfortable or secure, what impulse sent me in pursuit of the particular happiness denied to Don Miguel.

At Las Bordas a mule should have been waiting. The muleteer was asleep. Worse, it seemed that no mule was allowed to carry provisions into the mountains without a pass. Throughout the war the area between Andorra and the Pic du Midi d'Ossau had reverted to brigandage, and pockets of trouble had survived the peace. The sergeant who could frank our pass was away and the sergeant's wife who held the rubber stamp was naturally in bed. At last she was roused, the paper stamped, the mule loaded, and, as the first sun struck far above, we started into the mountains.

The air that morning as we walked up the valley of Artiga de Lin was fresh and cool. In its newness it was suited to a setting-out, to the beginning of adventure. Above the meadows, we climbed through beechwoods. There was no sound, except a tinkle as the mule's hoof struck a stone and at intervals a cry from the muleteer urging his beast. Straying to pick wild strawberries, we stumbled into a bear trap and were delighted that such hazards existed. When the woods grew brighter and insects glistered in flutes of slanting light, we realized that the sun had caught us. The day was moving on. But in this beechwood, time was palpable, innocent and open. It is always so, when one is committed to anything that seems worth doing. Only when the day, the week, the month, pass with no sense of reality, and their passage is barely registered in greying hairs, the friend estranged, the altered habit, does time presage death. It then moves like the cunning stalker in Grandmother's Steps. Eyes are covered; no one is near; yet as one turns the tap falls on one's shoulder. Time in activity, time valuable, is half disarmed. Never is one more free, yet aware, of time than in the mountains. There it never smoulders to the grey ash which marks the progress of a life-sentence. Time, the enemy-friend, is always present to the mountaineer. He works with it and against it. Each hour of daylight is valuable, and so is valued. Committed to the ridge or rock-face, even to the crossing of a simple Pyrenean pass such as was ours, he is interlocked with time. Success or failure depends upon it. His day moves closely with the sun. Time in the mountains is real and so is robbed of its penumbral horror. No one has aged climbing without the recognition that the change was fair and that time has taken no more than was paid for.

Near the tree-line the forest thinned. Fingers of light that seemed like transparent birches gave place to white obelisks, then to pools of sun, then to awkward gaps among the trees. Walking through dense woods one gains height without noticing, and the elation of being detached and above the world comes suddenly. Stepping from the last circle of shade, we found that our horizon had miraculously grown. We were on high pastures where immense yellow mullens made a new and miniature forest; wheatears and black redstarts watched us from outcrops of stone; we were on terms with a dozen lesser peaks. To the south rose the Poumera and the profile, so deceptively noble, of the Fourcanade that we were later to climb. Today our route swung west to the Col de l'Inferno. Treading the smooth turf of open pastures, we mounted voluptuous slopes that reposed in the clear air like vast female shapes under coverlets of green.

Crowning the last of these recumbent forms was the little Pic de l'Escalette. As we scrambled up the rocks the central Pyrenees unfolded. In one direction the velvet hills flowed down to France. Already the light was moulding the rounded shoulders and arms, and in the long green combes shadows were gathering. Eastward, far below, the curving trough of the Val d'Aran (meadows hedged with stunted trees, lean stone-roofed hamlets perched on hillsides) climbed to the valley's sculptured end at the Bonaigüe Pass. Beyond the pass, half the Pyrenees, peak on peak, stretched to the Mediterranean. Southward rose our immediate goal, the massif of the Aneto, draped with glaciers and glittering in the sun. Directly west, and so seen that the peaks backed one against another giving no sense of perspective, stretched the Atlantic half of the range, a jumble of shale, rock and snow.

On our small peak, we could appreciate the differing nature of the two faces of the Pyrenees. From the north in a few hours we had breasted the summit ridge of the chain, but southward, beyond the Pic d'Aneto, we could see ridge on ridge fading into blue distance. On the French side, the approach to the watershed is short and the geography simple. The range stands up boldly. Sometimes as little as twenty miles in a straight line separate the plain beyond the foothills and the summits at 11,000 feet. Ridges and buttresses jolting to these summits enclose short valleys, called *jasses*, with a characteristic stepped formation : stretches of upland pasture, almost level, that offer easy walking, they are separated by brief gorges where the water foams between walls of rock. Here in tedious zig-zag the mule tracks climb the mountain flanks. By contrast on the Spanish side it is often sixty miles from the plain to the watershed. Subsidiary ranges run parallel to the main chain, and the waters find their way to the Ebro by circuitous routes. Curiously enough it is also south of the watershed, as we could note from our vantage point, that the highest peaks, for obscure geological reasons, are found. This south is a deep and tangled area, little visited. Its isolation is increased by the surprising elevation of the passes which are higher than those in the Alps. When we first stood on the Pic de l'Escalette, there was no road across the range between the Bonaigüe Pass to the east and the Pourtalet westward, a distance of seventy-five miles.

The vegetation on the two sides of the Pyrenees was as different as their formation. The beechwoods through which we had climbed were characteristic of the northern slopes, where close forests mantle the mountainsides. In the country where we were bound, the 2,000 square miles between the Posets and the Encantados, between the streams of the Ara and the Noguera Pallaresa, trees were few and gnarled, and the climate drier; yet the region was pocked with small lakes, lending permanent surprise and freshness to the landscape, and the lower slopes were fantastically flowered.

An unlikely green ridge, thatched with turf, its sides steep as a gabled roof, led from our belvedere to the Col de l'Inferno. There was nothing forbidding about the pass on a June day, though in retrospect we seem to have carried our mule across the brief rocky passage. So we came to the Port de la Picarde, saw our first lammergeier with wing-span like an aeroplane, and found, between the massif of the Aneto and the main chain where we stood, the upper-most reach of the Val d'Esera cradled at our feet. Lying so, between glacier and rock, the gentleness of this remote valley, its winding stream, its air of seclusion, linked it with the idyllic pastures that shelter in the mind. It came as a gift, generously and unexpectedly. The sun slanting across the valley lent a liquid softness to the depths below us. We might have been looking into an unruffled lake, 2,500 feet of clear water. A mile distant, where the valley dropped away, the Esera made an elbow-turn to the south, thus giving the valley-head its secrecy. As so rarely happens in nature, we looked on a work of art. The very perfection was strange; such things do not normally come about. We felt for the first time that unreality, that sense of a landscape under spell, which travellers have repeatedly noted in these Pyrenees.

An alpine valley would have been groomed and put to use, beautiful in a different way: pastures subdivided into toy-like rectangles and rhomboids, tousled mops of hay drying on ash poles, ruminating cattle, brown chalets. Here there seemed no sign of life or husbandry, until our muleteer indicated, among the boulders on the opposing mountainside, the hut to which Don Miguel had secured the key, and drew our attention to a curious brown'blotch on the pastures below. 'Mares,' he said.

We descended knee-deep through feathery grasses. They parted easily, and we walked, scattering myriads of grass seeds, as through green foam. There were Turk's head lilies and patches of iris, islands of brilliant blue set capriciously in the green sea. Quail, unusual at such altitude, flushed at our feet, but their straight brusque flight, as always, lacked determination, and they collapsed into the grass fifty yards away. We were silent. One talks in a hut or by a fire in the open, but not much when walking or climbing: one is either too preoccupied, or too happy. Going down to the Val d'Esera we were happy.

Approaching the valley bottom we remarked that the hundreds of horses pasturing there did not stray. The brown blotch they made extended no more than a quarter mile, as though they were confined within this area by a mysterious social tie. They varied from cream to black, and these colours were seen against sward, the curve of each back outlined against the green. They were not mere quadrupeds, for they had the presence of the animals that obsessed Piero di Cosimo. Though sharing with the valley the permanence of art—and here again was strangeness—they seemed to wheel in continual movement about an invisible centre. This was the more surprising for when one looked closely, narrowing vision to ten square yards, one detected only a shaken mane, a lifted hoof, an occasional arbitrary turn. Our route brought us to the fringes of the herd and, as we threaded our way among them, I was glad that they disregarded us. They had grown larger, as landowners do on their own estates, and we seemed to reach only their withers. They were the aborigines of the valley, the proper owners, and intruding on their gathering we were lucky not to be challenged in an unknown language. We trod delicately among the cropping beasts, who so generously ignored us. They had, we found, a herdsman; that he, in his rags and with his domed mud-hovel, could perform some useful office for these noble creatures seemed improbable. Here at the headwaters of the Esera to be human was a disadvantage. Less confident than his herd, the man jumped to his feet and held a great staff like a barrier towards us. We spoke from a distance and he was still watching uncertainly (though of the herd not a head was lifted) as we moved from the soft nap of the valley to the boulder-strewn slopes of the Aneto. In half an hour we had reached the hut.

★   ★   ★

There is pleasure in an untenanted hut; in disposing one's gear methodically; in finding employment for hook, table, and bench, perhaps long unused; in starting a fire and creating warmth. The process offers the satisfaction of moving into a new house, but is accomplished in an hour. It is a satisfaction rarely to be enjoyed in the Spanish Pyrenees. We little realized that we slept that night in comfort such as existed nowhere else in Aragon at 7,000 feet. In an area which knew little of climbing history, of guides, guidebooks, or huts, the Aneto and the Rencluse Hut were exceptional. As the highest point of the Pyrenees, the Aneto had been attempted in the eighteenth century. It had been climbed in 1842 and, though lying well in Spanish territory, had for decades been a popular ascent. The logical approach was from Luchon; the frontier was crossed, and the Esera gained, by a dramatic notch in the watershed, the Port de Benasque, a passage between rock walls at some 8,000 feet. Before the first hut was built, people made their bivouac and lit their fires in a cave-like shelter, 'la Rencluse'. Later a cabin was built near by, where the amiable and rugged Madame Sayo, whose reputation has long outlived her, ministered to mountaineers. Time passed. With the Civil War the frontier was closed and those who found their way into the region did not come to climb. When the authorities regained control of the area, after 1945, the Rencluse was in ashes. It had been rebuilt by José Abadias, whom we were later to meet, patriarch and innkeeper at Benasque, six hours down the Esera valley. Thus we slept under a roof.

We woke to storm and wind, but even these can be acceptable in a quiet hut, if days are not too precious. There is a frayed rope-end to re-bind and crumpled flowers to identify. Beside the stove we pored over maps; we talked of other mountains and augured hopefully from other storms on other occasions; we dozed over our books; we slept. Intermittently we questioned the barometer and from the window looked at the struggle above, watched the battle sway as the peaks threw off the assaulting cloud or went down fighting, blotted out. When it cleared towards evening, our spirits lifted like the vapour. We stepped out buoyantly to find the air deliciously clear, rinsed by the departed rain and wind. Jumping like children from boulder to boulder, we raced along the mountainside. Above us the peaks, hidden all day, had returned firm and confident to their stations. The valley glistened, no longer obscured by veils of driving rain. The mares in their formal circle were grazing unconcerned as ever, and the herdsman was fishing on the bank of the stream. Beside him an enormous white Pyrenean sheep-dog sat on its haunches.

That evening we would not have been elsewhere at any price. Though the weather was perhaps a little too warm, the stars were out. Tomorrow we should climb the Aneto. In itself the climb was nothing, *un nada* as someone had airily remarked in the café at Lés. But here in Aragon there were no reassuring tracks, no guidebooks or maps as the modern climber knows them. Imagination was free to play on our 11,000-foot mountain. We were back in the nineteenth century and this constituted the very point of our expedition. Having set the alarm-clock for three-thirty, we should have crawled early into our sleeping-bags, but already the morning was with us in anticipation, making sleep difficult. We poured more wine and sat talking at the trestle table, while the stove purred. Naturally we talked of the Aneto, the inelegant but convincing massif that couched above us in the dark. Draped with glaciers it stretched three miles from the Pic d'Alba to the Pic des Tempêtes, and the summit ridge dropped nowhere below 10,000 feet. We already knew something of our route, but in the vaguest terms. Immediately south of the hut rose the Pic de la Maladetta, and its glacier, tied like a napkin round its neck, was 2,000 feet above us. From this peak a spine of rock, bordering the Maladetta glacier, fell without inter-ruption to the headwaters of the Esera and the level pastures below us; it cut the massif effectively in two, separating the Maladetta glacier from the larger Aneto glacier on the east. This rocky spine was easily accessible from our side, but it overhung the Aneto glacier and there was only one convenient point of traverse known as the *portillon*. Thence the route led up the Aneto glacier. Over two miles broad, it was little crevassed, yet I remembered that on an early expedition the guide Barrau had cried, 'I sink, I sink.' A century had not brought him to the surface. Crossing the glacier diagonally we should reach, beyond the final *Bergschrund* and the glistening white dome above, the acute rock ridge, sixty yards of granite, that leads to the summit. Known as the Pont de Mahomet, the ridge presumably derived its name from the rope known to Muslim theology which stretches over hell and which the righteous alone can cross to attain Paradise. The name was no stranger than that of the Maladetta, the Accursed Mountain. 'Accursed' they say because Christ wandering in this wilderness, and meeting with fierce herdsmen and fiercer dogs, turned the latter to stone. Christ, Mahomet, such are the names that shepherds here have long invoked.

To talk of the Aneto was also to talk of the two friends to whom, in a sense, the massif and much of the Pyrenees rightfully belong. We envisaged them, clad in Norfolk jackets, perhaps wearing the new-fangled balaclava helmets, on the skyline at the *portillon*, or straddling the Pont de Mahomet. By the wheezing stove in the Rencluse it was a duty to remember them, for no mountain chain has been so lovingly pioneered as were the central Pyrenees by Packe and Russell. They discovered most of the region nearly a century ago. Having no maps, with no guide but observation and a compass, year after year they navigated like sailors among the unknown reefs and glaciers. Their first ascents are numberless; it was *their* country. Perhaps for this reason, their expeditions were not assaults. They did not conquer peaks to possess and leave them, as do mountain philanderers. Their climbs were not a battle and a parting: they cherished their mountains and returned. Packe climbed the Aneto six times; Russell, who made at least five ascents, once spent a night on the summit and at dawn noted the snow blood-red where the first sun struck, but deep blue in the shadows.

Though friends, they were different, representing two approaches to the mountains on which mountaineering has much depended, the scientific and the romantic. Charles Packe was geologist, botanist, cartographer, and scholar (climbing with Horace in his pocket). He was also the squire of Stretton Hall, the Leicestershire gentleman who found the Pyrenees more exciting than the hunting field. Much of this was concealed by a brusque manner, for though a modest man he was not an easy one. He began his systematic exploration of the chain in 1859. When a companion was killed on the Pic de Sauvegarde in the same year, while no doubt perturbed, he was clearly not deflected. Noting Jurassic limestone, greensand, names of rare flowers, barometric pressures, and making in the uncharted country expedition on expedition, he accumulated knowledge. It found expression in the first guide-book to the central Pyrenees and the first map of the Maladetta area. At this remove the methodical explorer allows a single welcome glimpse of the eccentric squire: on solitary expeditions he roped with Ossoüe and Azor, his great Pyrenean sheepdogs. Thus a hundred years ago, but surely in misplaced confidence, he crossed a frozen tarn, and perhaps negotiated the icefields of the Aneto.

'Mon ami Packe', the phrase recurs throughout the writings of Count Henri Patrick Marie Russell-Killough. The latter's was an affectionate and generous character. Born in France, and heir to a papal title, Russell was an Irish Catholic. These facts were less important to him than the works of Chateaubriand, Lamartine, and Byron, and the mountains which he always saw in some part through their eyes. His life was a late but heroic expression of the romantic era. From that era both his literary style—for he had weird but considerable talent as a writer—and his attitudes derived much of their bravura. Charm, passion, eccentricity, created his legend; there have been many less well founded. As a young man he wrote verse, played the fiddle, and would dance all night ('effréné valseur' they said) before starting on a thirty-mile walk at dawn. His romantic daemon sent him briefly and disastrously to sea, and led him in his early twenties happily across Siberia, to Australia, to New Zealand (where he was lost for three days in the Alps alone and without food), to the Americas, and even to within sight of Everest. On his return in 1863, at the age of twenty-nine, he first climbed the Aneto and met Packe. The rest of his life was, quite simply, devoted to the Pyrenees.

The range brought him something like European fame. He made at least sixteen first ascents, and it is in character that many of them should have been solitary. On the other hand his contribution to the scientific knowledge of the chain was negligible. It would have been illogical to expect otherwise. In his writings, above all in *Souvenirs d'un Montagnard*, he made a different contribution, an eloquent apology for an emotional approach to mountains. The Pyrenees that claimed him were not Packe's. 'Je respecte', he wrote, 'et j'envie ceux pour qui la montagne est autre chose qu'une idole. Je suis jaloux de ceux que la géodésie, l'anatomie des pics et l'éclimètre, passionnent autant que la voix des torrents, le pourpre des précipices, et l'incendie des neiges au coucher du soleil. Mais à chacun son rôle. . . . Le mien fut de marcher et de sentir.'

The Count's almost obsessive feeling for the Pyrenees found its most satisfying expression in his relationship with the Vignemale. This reads like some complicated love affair. Rising in the Grand Vignemale, the highest peak of the French Pyrenees, to 10,820 feet, provided with the most shapely glacier in the range and some of the most forbidding precipices, the mountain held him from childhood. He reached its summit thirty-three times, making his last ascent at the age of seventy. Long before then he had felt the need to achieve a closer and more prolonged contact with the Vignemale than was possible by mere mountaineering. Nothing would satisfy but a home not far from the summit, where he could if necessary live for days at a time and know his mountain in all seasons, and in storm as well as settled weather. The idea of building among palaces of ice, schist, and marble, seemed impertinent. A grotto was the only acceptable solution: 'Une œuvre humaine, mais qui n'en eût pas l'air, et où on ne devinerait pas la main de l'homme: en un mot un abri qui eût l'air naturel.'

No one knew better than Count Russell that a grotto was not to be found on the Vignemale. He decided to carve his own from solid rock. In the summer of 1880 he began to look for a site, and in the course of his search spent the night of August 16th on the Grand Vignemale in most curious circumstances. As light began to fail, his two companions, peasant-mountaineers from Gavarnie, were instructed to dig a grave upon the summit. Then, laid out in his sheep-skin bag, he gave orders for his burial. Having covered him to the neck in a cumbrous blanket of stone and soil, his companions retreated to shelter some way below the summit. With a vivid anticipation of pleasure, the Count awaited the night and the cold. 'L'ami Packe' one feels would not have approved such eccentricity.

A few hundred feet beneath the buried Count a still and level sea of cloud stretched from horizon to horizon. At times he seemed already to have left the earth and to be floating above it; at others to be watching from a last rocky eminence the earth's slow and final inundation. When the moon rose shortly before midnight the ocean of cloud, as though the light infected it with fever, began to stir and shudder. There was now unceasing agitated movement that threw up plumes of grey spray and hurled breakers against invisible shoals. Yet the cloud level did not rise; even, as the night wore on, it began to sink and, like the retreating Flood, rendered up one dripping summit after another. All this apparently in a windless silence, as unnatural as death. The temperature dropped to − 3 degrees centigrade and a hoar frost whitened the grave and the Count's pointed beard. What, he wondered, would have been the effect on some benighted mountaineer, chancing to find on such a summit a frozen decapitated head? Madness, he concluded, and fell asleep.

This night may be regarded as the last dedicated vigil of his novitiate; it was prelude to long and arduous possession of the mountain. The chosen site for his grotto was in the wall of rock that bars the head of the Ossoüe glacier at 10,500 feet. The vagaries of the glacier were later to present an unexpected challenge; meanwhile for two summers there was a coming and going along its crevassed length of peasants and miners, carrying explosives, wood and food. The haul was made from the village of Gèdre over 7,000 feet below, and the Count always superintended from the most advanced positions. Sometimes the glacier was in thick mist and they moved slowly, step by step, among the crevasses. Sometimes plastered in falling snow, the flakes large as florins, they looked like white statues. Sometimes they fought foot by foot against the wind. More than other mountains in the range, the Vignemale has a reputation for great storms. They dossed down, all of them, under a large heavily-tarred canvas. Tools broke, the explosives got wet, but by the beginning of August 1882 the grotto was ready.

The first night was spent there with his friend, Francis Swan. They slept comfortably on hay; without a fire the temperature was 7 degrees centigrade. In the following year Miss Swan became the first lady visitor. The owner was beginning to settle in. It is curious to watch the splendid obsession grow, the sojourns in the grotto multiply in number and length. Three days, four days, nine days. . . . He makes neighbours; the snow finches begin to rely on his visits. From his doorstep, he saves two young English mountaineers, lost and exhausted, who have fallen into a crevasse. Mass is celebrated in the grotto by the Abbé Pomès. Some of the thirty who attend kneel on the glacier outside, and the snow about them is reddened by the dawn. Soon a single grotto is not enough. In 1885 the *Grotte des Guides* follows, in 1886 the modest *Grotte des*

Dames. The possession of the mountain seems complete. As though to celebrate the fact an extraordinary scene is enacted, recalling an Arabian banquet displaced in temperature and altitude. The Comte de Monts (significant name) appears with friends and a capacious tent rises on the glacier before the grottoes. Columns sculptured in frozen snow flank its entrance and the approach is a lawn of red lichens, *Silene acaulis* and *Androsace carnea*. Persian carpets are spread and white napery. They decant the vintage wines and carve the huge *jambon de Bayonne*, looking in its coat of fat like a marble boulder; reclining on cushions they burn oriental perfumes and smoke long Havana cigars. There is not air enough to sway even the lanterns, and for three days the barometer is steady.

But the Vignemale demanded more of this lover. In 1887 the glacier began to stir, as the cloud ocean had stirred, but slowly rising against the rock face, lapping steadily higher. The lower grottoes disappeared like foundered ships. Only the *Grotte des Dames* remained accessible. With unbroken spirit but something like a broken heart, the Count withdrew from his advanced position to just under 7,900 feet. There in 1888 at the foot of the Ossoüe glacier a new grotto was hollowed out of the mountain. *Bellevue* faced south, and a spring for the first time made him independent of melted snow-water. Two ancillary grottoes followed. With their Freudian overtones, there is something desperate about these penetrations, these determined acts of love. But the true object of veneration was now 3,000 feet above; *Bellevue* seemed like the plain, and Russell sat there longing for the harsh

43

glare of snow, the lammergeiers, and the precipices. By 1892 he felt his position intolerable; the more so since the mountain had now for some years been *his*. The seven surrounding communes had, with imagination, legalized his relationship, presenting him with the four summits of the Vignemale and the glacier that flowed down to his door.

To seal his devotion he determined, with a supreme effort, to build his last and seventh grotto at the summit of the Grande Vignemale itself. Four men worked for over a month in vain. Only when he brought up dynamite in 1893 was the thing accomplished and the Count lodged at nearly 10,820 feet. *Le Paradis* also faced south and proved beautifully dry. It was the reward of a long and ardent attachment, surely one of the most intense in the history of mountaineering. There, in his sixtieth year, he celebrated in his own phrase the 'silver wedding' of his first ascent.

*   *   *

I slept fitfully. Several times I woke, fumbled for my watch, and mistook moonlight for dawn. At last I must have sunk deep, like the sleepers of Lès, for I found R. shaking me. Chilly and morose, we had neither appetite for coffee by the light of a candle, nor for the coming day. The mountain seemed to tower above us. It was four-thirty when we pushed open the door and stepped without conviction into the night.

The moon had set, but at our feet was the pale indication of a track. Where it ceased, we each took our own route upward. In the half-light R. was a drifting ghost, material only in the clink of her ice-axe on the boulders. We crossed a glacier stream. Though shrunken by the night's frost, it seemed to thunder in the surrounding silence and its raucous course glittered as if its motion attracted the scattered light from a shadowy landscape. Later came the familiar blessing, the second awakening on a mountainside and the sense of a drowsy life sloughed in the hut below. As in the early mornings of youth, one then becomes part of the day not yet begun, of a future, of possibility. One breathes the still cold air and has no inkling that later one will certainly be tired, possibly dispirited or defeated. There is nothing but confidence.

At some point dawn was with us, its coming unperceived. The stars had gone. The grass at our feet, the flowers though closed and retracted, even the rocks and their lichens, held hidden colour. It was still in suspense, a promise merely, but the anonymity of night had passed. Eastward a small cloud turned pink and a wash of sky was slit by a line of mountains sharp as a knife. Above us the obscure thing that held our imagination took shape, became a peak. Upon its flank was tumbled a wilderness of boulders, Christ's savage dogs long turned to stone. We clambered into the morning through this grey necropolis. As distances grew, we lessened to dots in an expanding landscape. A breeze fluttered off the white napkin of the Maladetta glacier. We set foot on the lowest tongue of ice not much before sunrise.

When we reached the spine of rock that separates the Maladetta and Aneto glaciers, the sun was warm on our backs. Our position between the two ice-sheets was splendid. Seated on a knobbly vertebra of rock we appeared to occupy the precise centre of a newly revealed world. The solitary turning earth had, it seemed in an hour, drawn from darkness the clear and scintillating planes and spaces that now surrounded us. Immediately below lay the Aneto glacier and no crevasse marred the sparkling expanse of snow. The steep slope leading to the Pont de Mahomet gleamed as innocently beyond and its guardian *Bergschrund* offered convenient points of traverse. It was a moment to prolong.

Only later did we look in vain for the *portillon*, the passage which offers descent to the Aneto glacier. Easy and inviting the glacier stretched away, yet appeared unattainable. The distance was just too great for descent on a doubled rope. Like animals in some white Whipsnade, deprived of freedom by a single effective ditch, we scuttled up and down the rock-rib, peering over the edge. As later transpired, we had climbed too high in the careless rhythm of early morning and the *portillon* lay a thousand feet lower.

When we at last gained the glacier, the sun was hot and the snow softening. We had expected a frozen surface for the slogging traverse. Valuable time had been lost, but the sky was clear and even the small pink cloud had disappeared. The summit of the Pyrenees seemed easily ours. As we trudged upward the neighbouring peaks rose into view. Propelled skyward by that silent well-oiled machinery which operates in the mountains, they made their dignified appearances without effort and always where least expected. I would raise my eyes from the glacier to find a new and detached observer, still and un-ruffled as though not lately arrived from Aragon or Béarn. I often have this impression of being watched by the mountains, and according to my circumstances it can either elevate or disquiet. These cool critics of our progress, of two labouring ants discovered in their range of vision, may have relished the hour that followed.

One does not think of wind. At first staccato buffets arrived, as though a giant *putto* with monstrously distended cheeks provoked us. Then, out of a steel-blue sky, a gale poured down the glacier. We swam against a violent current, caught in a mill-race that swept to the ice-falls below. Our rope tugged and bellied, struggling to escape. Repeatedly the gale caught us with raised foot and sent us staggering. Almost drowned for lack of the breath that was snatched from our lips, we would halt, twisting from the gale, to take deep gulps of air. Sometimes on this white tilted river-bed, our ice-axes alone maintained us against the current, like stakes that a failing swimmer might have grasped. Never out of a candid sky have I known such an attack. Launched in clear sunlight it was doubly disconcerting for we seemed the object of calculated onslaught. More than once we thought of turning back. Then, suddenly as it had begun, the flood weakened. There was no longer a pressure on our chests; our arms grew lighter and we could inscribe gestures on the air; we could stand upright. We seemed like survivors from the bursting of a huge barometric dam.

As we crossed the terminal crevasse and left the glacier, the last trickling breeze died away. The impredictability of

47

mountains becomes lovable. They never declare their hands, and this is an accepted element of the relationship. Thus their treacheries are fair deception, half expected, and met without bitterness. At lower levels the sudden veering of affection and prejudice, the silver that slumps in the heart's barometer, are always a surprise and find one unprepared. The gale had come without warning, was accepted, and now we were simply glad that it had gone. The white dome rose steeply in a welcome stillness. After the maelstrom we were conscious of the smallest sounds: the 'tchug, tchug' of boots kicking foothold in the snow, the rustle of an anorak, the whisper of our breath. We could also use our eyes again with pleasure, perceive the granulation of the snow, the suave moulding of the white shoulder before us, the small inverted cones of blue shadow impressed by our axe-points, and our own shadows wrapped, now that the sun was high, closely about our feet.

The Pont de Mahomet which had promised to be the crux of the day proved an airy scramble on beautifully firm granite. Mountains that launch gales offer such charities. A small crucifix, marking the spot where a party had been struck by lightning, reminded us that the place would be very different in bad weather. Across the 'bridge' we found ourselves on the top of the Pyrenees.

A summit that has called for a day's effort gives in return a brief, no more than brief, trance of achievement. Description has been attempted in the language of mysticism and of love, but it had better be left alone. The moment soon passes. That is among its characteristics. We became busied with trivia: finding a nook for the rucksack and a knob for

48

the rope, easing boots, settling down. It was as if we sought to do such things, and do them soon, to avoid being confronted with the fact that the mountain had been climbed, that a goal had been reached and therefore no longer existed. We had looked to find something—doubtless something we had brought ourselves, yet still important—and after a moment we were merely sitting, rather tired, on a few shattered rocks. The geological reality is always inadequate. It could not be otherwise.

Later there succeeded a tempered elation. It was in this mood that we got to our feet and scrutinized the upward route, now permanently ours though thousands of other boots might scrape the rock and dirty the snow. In this mood we looked about and gathered to us, even in the knowledge that the picture would never be altogether clear again, the constellation of peaks and the depths of air. This sober elation is of a sort that keeps. A modest thing and reliable, it may be summoned at sea-level by the simple act of memory. It will combat, as surely as art does or faith is said to do, the horror of *accedia*. In moments of no hope, it comes out with sensible affirmation; it says, 'You are wrong and you know you are wrong, because on such and such a mountain' (and elements of the scene return) 'even you could recognize that the nonsensical jumble of experience was well patterned.'

In the Alps the great peaks often jostle in shouldering competition. In its relative isolation the Aneto overlooked all Spain and most of France. From the north, white cumulus advanced, curling top-heavy breakers always about to plunge. They came on, yet never broke, or breasted (such is the habit of these clouds forming over Béarn) the abrupt frontier chain. To the south, far below us, lay the remote valley of Malibierne with its enormous tortured conifers. Their writhing forms were scattered a day's march down scree and boulder to distant feathery pastures and the glint of water. We could see no habitation, no sign of flock or shepherd. Range on range stretched into Aragon, each mountain flank washed with haze and indeterminate, but the line of each indigo ridge-crest carefully drawn. Beyond the last ridge one sensed rising heat from the plain of the Ebro. But chiefly we looked, as to a promised land, where a tangle of peaks trended eastward. Though we could not identify the Encantados, we knew that their signature was part of the crowded text on the horizon.

II
THE APPROACH

Two days later we abandoned the Rencluse hut, and turned
unaccountably westward. It was one of many elaborate yet
leisurely detours, ceremonious retreats and advances, which
kept us, at the least, a safe day's journey from the Encantados. These wanderings, and they were little more, on the
Spanish side of the Pyrenees have left a lasting flavour in
the memory.

Our first camp, and it was like many others, lay in a
high-slung cradle between the frontier ridge and the
isolated mass of the Posets, a white eruption against the
parched distances of Aragon. The site was turf-covered,
and the turf in places hardly visible for flowers; there was
a stream, at this cradle stage, still moving collectedly from
one sand-fringed pool to another; there were tenacious
pines, solitary outposts, that on the limits of the tree-line
were as individual as people. Snow-drifts lay in the hollows, and above us the flank of the frontier ridge was
streaked black and white like a zebra. Wind, stripping the
rocks, had piled fluid stripes of snow in all the sheltered
lees and troughs.

We had walked in the cool of early morning through
chestnut and alder, through mazes of scented box; we had
looked into gorges, where our stream, fulminating between
rock walls, hurtled down to join the Esera. We might have

stopped anywhere, but we approved one favouring patch of ground. There the mule was unloaded. Our bales looked stranded and defenceless in the landscape, until the ritual of pitching camp, of establishing human order in the wildness, gave them significance. This making camp is the play of children, and as satisfactory. Of nothing a habitation is created: the tent faces south; a cellar is established in the shade; the kitchen shelters in the lee of a big rock; the laundry is beside the stream; firewood is collected, stacked, and covered with a tarpaulin. The mule and his flies are stabled some way off. Persons and bales by the mere exercise of nursery logic are safely settled. There is an encampment.

After sunset as the heights above us slowly drifted away and then were gone, the circle of light thrown by the fire became our extreme horizon. But for a few yards of turf, and a few boulders against which our gear was conveniently propped, the landscape disappeared; the encampment alone remained. Sitting late, idly feeding the flames, we were the centre of silence. Yet mountains except in severe frost are rarely silent; even at night the silence is in oneself. If one listens there are stones shifting uneasily on the moraine, the trickle of melting snow, somewhere distantly a torrent, and the discreet sough of air creeping down the couloirs, picking at the closed flowers, passing through gaps in the pines, spilling steadily from the high plateaux and the lips of mountain cradles such as ours. Reaching the sleeping villages on the edge of the plain it breathes the smell of snow into bedrooms. At dawn the process is reversed. The tide that ebbed all night returns, bearing cattle and men upward to work in high pastures, drowning them and passing on, seeping into the bare uplands until it brims level with the peaks. One inhales on the *névé* at noon air that lay before dawn on vineyards. It is still heavy with valley dew and a fine perception might register the scent of hay, of loam, of dung, of striped melons ripening in stone-walled plots. This repeated ebb and flow became a part of our existence. Storms and their cataclysms were brief interruptions; the mountains breathed and the daily tide rose and fell.

In the Pyrenees one can sleep in the open with comfort at 7,000 feet, and we spread our swansdown bags that first night to windward of the fire. Waking, I threw a branch on the ashes, watched it catch, and dozed off with flames leaping and pushing back the circle of darkness. Before dawn we left for some mountain top of which I have no particular recollection. Often the precise occasions of this time are indistinct. There were a few dawns that never occurred, when light all day filtered indistinctly through grey muslin or reached us as a flicker of swirling snow; days, more often, when the sun shone for twelve hours. Memory is equally confused by the mist, and by the reflection from metallic rocks and glaring snow. Returning late across velvet slopes to stream or wood, our marching shadows are uniformly long and thin and cannot be easily assigned to a day or place. It is a taste of newness, a distillation of freshness, that remains. Every day was a long discovery that carried its bloom to the moment when I nodded by the fire and was snuffed out in sleep. We escaped our familiar stationary selves, and the resulting freedom, the illusion of moving significantly onward, gave to all progress in these mountains a heady charm. This illusion is the property of youth, its sign manual, and with its return we seemed unaged.

There was daily entry with eye, foot, and hand, to fresh valleys, slopes and summits. The newness, the sense of constant unfolding, lay partly in the very nature of mountain landscape. As we moved upward, each day saw change from pasture and chestnut to pine and close turf, and so to rock and snow. From hour to hour we lost and gained flowers, while even the same species deepened in colour at higher altitude and the very sky slowly assumed a darker hue, hinting at the night of the stratosphere. Each day presented both abundance and astringency. Starting, usually at sunrise, from a green and copious nature, we left some facet of its rich variety at every step, only to find ourselves paradoxically richer for the spareness of snow and rock that lifted our spirits. The reward of return was as great, for we seemed to have forgotten the varied wealth below. The easy-growing flowers, the niched ferns, water dripping over moss, and the first tree, came as our sudden pleasure.

Even perspective was a constant surprise; things looked, as they always do in the mountains, different from above and below. A pocket-handkerchief of snow, our mark 2,000 feet higher, would prove a wide expanse of *névé* where we kicked laborious steps; a rock-tower on a distant ridge would move unobtrusively to meet us and reappear a brief rope's length away; an inviting rib that seemed firmly attached to the spine of our mountain would withdraw, confounding us with a gulf where choughs swirled.

The same route was unrecognizable on different days. An approach over angry scree, where I had first climbed wrapped in thought, would seem on another occasion interminable, or a passage, once forbidding, would be re-crossed without pause. Often the very feel and texture of the same rocks would change. The mountains were remade each day.

Perhaps because of the immense setting, detail was arrestingly vivid. I would be confronted by a flower (and this happened most often when it appeared on a ledge at eye-level) that seemed utterly new though I had seen the species a hundred times. 'Look,' I would say, my eyes free of the grey cataract of habit, 'there is a new flower.' The presentation was immediate. Given the remoteness of these hills, there was indeed a sense in which it had never been seen before and probably never would be seen again. For the first and only time the flower and a human being were confronted. I sometimes had the odd feeling that the meeting had been awaited by the flower and was not of significance only to me. Again, we would both stare in amazement at lichens, a handwriting momentarily un-familiar, or pause in wonder at the wrack of a dead pine that was like dozens we had seen. With delight we noticed butterflies on a scrap of marshy ground, the familiar bird balanced on a twist of juniper, or the velvet surface of a stream in which I sunk my gurgling waterbottle. Such awareness seemed proof of new relationships.

There was also a pool. Yet pool is too pretending a word. This was a little water with the clarity of dew left by melt-ing snow on a mountain shoulder and cupped on the lip of nothing. Though so clear, I could not easily see *into* it, for sky and curling white cumulus were there. Growing on the water's edge, the small blue gentian and a flower I could not name were also reflected in its margins. Only by breaking the surface could I have properly seen its soppy bottom, the same turf on which the flowers grew, for this was temporary water to be sucked away by the summer heat. Sitting without turning my head, I could look one way at the pool and the other into space. I and the pool were in the evening sun, but the valley lay in shadow. Observed against this shadow, an eagle was absorbedly circling, and contrast made the bird shine as an insect shines in a ray of sunlight. Though I could see its wingtips ruffled by a light breeze, none reached the mountainside. On the surface of the pool, unbroken, the only movement was that of drifting clouds.

When two bucketfuls of water could so speak, the peaks that began as names, points on dream-inducing maps, or non-committal statements against the sky-line, were bound to develop personalities. They were not the great personalities of the Alps, removed from intimacy, like the figures of history, by the aura of fame. They were contemporaries, persons with whom it was simple to establish contact. Though withholding the quick clear confessions of bird or lichen, they gave away much. A few were friable, sluttish and unkempt, always falling to pieces and leaving one with the same sense of discomfort as an unformed character. Some with a mixed geological inheritance showed, as people do, good strains and bad, both unalterable. Some veered like weathercocks: one day bland and friendly, but on return distant and grim. Some were boring. Some, that we sensed boastful and unrewarding, were better not visited. But some could not disappoint; propinquity revealed no flaw. These were the cherished mountains. One wears a regal toque of snow, another an iron helmet, another a skirt of green trees and a girdle of blue shale, and yet another, perhaps the best, a vein of white quartz across its breast like the ribbon of the Saint Esprit. They were often beautiful, for beauty of form in mountains is usually allied to character; and often they were varied, revealing at each pitch, or sequence of pitches, some new facet, some new delight. I think of them, and name them to myself, like proved friends for whom feelings cannot change. And across the next valley there was always the unclimbed mountain, the possibility of a further relationship. We would avidly con the map, strike camp, and set out afresh.

Our climbs for the most were not serious undertakings, and at this distance the weeks have become a distillation in which particular occasions and mountains tend to be lost. The days that survive as a clear-cut slice of time are few, and their survival often inexplicable. One such day was little more than a morning; yet it remains complete when other occasions, not unlike it, are irretrievably lost. The early scentless air was buoyant, and we walked towards the rising sun as though invisibly supported. From boulder to boulder we followed a stream to its source. There were pools with sides smoothly whorled by the tug of the water; rooted in the rocks, rowans and flowering bushes overhung miniature waterfalls. From two improbable lakes, each the length of a cricket pitch, rose islands where grew white rhododendron. As the stream shrunk, its course steepened. Soon it was slipping down faulted rocks, or hanging for curved moments in space, as though poured from the lips of successive jugs. We followed until it became a runnel in a granite groove, a sliding film on a slab, a dampness, nothing. So it led us insensibly into our climb. Above was delectable rock, warmed by the sun, and provided with precisely the right number of holds, neither too many nor too few. Each movement was pleasure and we seemed to move gracefully. The last half-hour that took us to the top—an anonymous point, a mere knob on a ridge—gave as much happiness as I expect to find. The summit was comfortable, and on our backs in the sun for the rest of that memorable morning we slept.

Danger, which is the myrrh and cassia of events, the sure embalmer, played little part in our wandering. Yet two of the occasions which remain owe something of their precision, spot-lit in memory, to the urgency of risk. The first was on the Fourcanade. We started before dawn for the hanging valley where the Alta Ribagorzana, that stream I love, issues modest and remote from a string of small lakes. They are snow-covered for nine months of the year, and in high summer a frenetic display of wild flowers borders the snow. At the head of the hanging valley, where there had anciently been yet another lake, a shallow bowl, its soil still holding moisture, was an extravagant garden. We pushed knee-deep through yellow gentian. Yet the walk was not agreeable. Even before sunrise we were sweating, bathed in hot puffs of sirocco that climbed with us from the south, and the pull over scree above the hanging valley seemed long. Stepping through a nick in the summit ridge, our reward was the snowy Cirque de Los Negros and the elegant shape of the Fourcanade. Unaware of our presence a troupe of izard proceeded sedately westward.

The Fourcanade seemed too good a mountain to ascend by the easy route. We accordingly crossed the Cirque to the foot of the east ridge which rose to the summit in an unbroken sweep. The heat was stifling. The tired air that reached us had taken no chill in its passage across the snow. Only the first few pitches of our climb looked awkward. We had not taken into account the nature of the rock. The mountain, as I have said, was elegant and the east ridge, like a blade, separated the vast precipices on the north from the respectable depths above the Cirque. Experience led us to expect good things of so narrow a crest; the fact that it was there at all, that it had so long resisted, seemed to promise solid rock. It proved inconceivably rotten. When I began to move upward, holds, big as footballs, came away in my hands. This perhaps was fair climbing hazard, for which wariness should be safeguard. It is moreover a hazard natural to the unfrequented routes of the Spanish Pyrenees, where the detritus of frost and weather are not cleared by human traffic. But on the Fourcanade, as though loosened by earthquake, the ridge itself, the very mountain, was unstable. Angry fissures pierced the heart of the ridge, implying rock-falls not to be measured. Enormous slabs groaned and eased themselves at the lightest pressure; towers rocked at a finger's touch; flakes the size of a giant turtle lurched dizzily outward at the mere passage of the rope. In the soupy puffs of the sirocco the whole mountain seemed to totter. A mass of rock, imposing as a throne, swayed idiotically and headed into space. As the tons shuddered downward they crashed fragmenting from one impact to another. Only specks like pebbles reached and dirtied the snow below, but an acrid dust, smelling of gunpowder, hung about the face of the precipice.

The first hour was like climbing in a Pompeian nightmare. The earth itself, the last friend, the only stable element in one's existence, seemed to have deserted to the enemy. A mountaineer has no right to trust a hold, but it is frightening to find that the frame, the very architecture, of nature is loose. Higher, where the angle of the ridge lessened, the rock improved. But we had become so used to instability that we moved gingerly, whispering down the rope, and gravely testing enormous blocks that were palpably solid. Infected with distrust, we swayed and fumbled, as unreliable as the ridge. Long before we flung ourselves on the flattened crown of the mountain (where happily nothing could fall off), we were unnerved.

The second occasion which a touch of fear has preserved with all its detail, a clear and complete occasion, was on the Pic d'Oo. Making at first through scattered pines, and then steeply beside a gorge and waterfall that sprayed us coldly as we climbed, we emerged on scree and the shrinking southern *névés*. I recorded in my diary, 'Joy of gaining height steadily before the sun rises.' By eight we were at a gap in the frontier ridge below the peak. Much of the impact of the Pyrenees lies in the contrast between the sun-baked southern slopes, where even in June the snow-drifts gasp like stranded fish, and the steeper northern faces, sometimes laced with glaciers, white and metallic. This contrast we now enjoyed. The north face of the Pic d'Oo dropped, perhaps 2,000 feet, to a grim lake where the wind shunted slabs of snow-covered ice. The lake is never free. Across this arctic foreground, France lay in sunlight.

On beautiful granite we scrambled to the summit. But the day was rapidly changing. The sun soon had gone. The sky, lately empty but for a distant bank of cloud, was obscured by milling waves of grey. We crouched below this stormy sea that rode louring over the peak and flecked us, as isolated snowflakes fell, with gobbets of spume. The change was annoying but posed no problem. We could safely retreat as we had come. We chose to do nothing of the sort. Traversing the peak, we decided to cross the north face above the icy lake and so regain the ridge that we had left in sunshine barely an hour before. The face, a mixture of shale and rock not unduly steep, might in good conditions have been little more than a walk. The conditions were not good: the scree was a sheet of ice, too thin to allow the cutting of effective steps, and masked with unstable snow. Yet we went. The decision to me is full of interest. I have spoken of mountains 'watching' the climber. There are days when they participate, guiding his hands, leading him to the hidden couloir, the only possible line of ascent. There are others—and this was one of them—when they simply watch, as the Fates watch, without interference, allowing a perverse flaw of judgement to work itself out. If they act at all, it is by inducing a blindness that leads inexorably from error to error.

The mountaineer has the impression of shaking off the

drugged responses of normal life, the false judgements which commit slowly and fatally to the discipline of courses and persons neither relevant nor fruitful. The impression is often, but not always, true. We had foreseen the storm; we had appreciated the state of the north face; yet we took our decision. I recall every yard of that glassy traverse, so easily avoidable, the look of the lake below with its casual icebergs, and the snow driving almost level in the gale. Even the gap in the ridge when we reached it was a howling funnel. The storm had given it weird decoration. Driving snow, wherever it found purchase, had drawn out feather-like shapes, cold plumes a foot long. A giant plucking-machine had been at work, scattering on the rocks frozen shakos and the wing-feathers of geese. We staggered at last southward out of the gale, each step taking us further from the icy slopes and an experience which we had not wanted, yet seemed clearly to have courted. Lower the snow fell more gently, mantling the long southern screes, thatching with white the dwarf rhododendrons, the *Rhododendron ferruginosa* of these mountains. As we reached our tent and the snow changed to drizzle (looking back we saw the white storm-fall like an inverted tide-line along the mountain flank), I was still confronting the gut-deep blindness that obscures judgement impredictably on mountains and in drawing-rooms.

That evening we sat pondering. We could both recall another day when a thread, that seemed specially spun, drew us fully conscious into a situation equally unpleasant. It had been in the Italian Alps. The first sun met our party of four—and two were mountaineers of great experience—as we reached the foot of the climb. Though the summit was shrouded in drifting pink cloud, our ridge stretched upward with all the invitation of good rock, solid as though poured from a mould that morning. There was no wind, and the rock was warm to touch. With the proviso that we kept to the crest of the ridge and avoided the north face, it promised pleasure but no serious difficulties. On the north face the rocks, by contrast, were dangerously glazed and the precipitous ice slopes covered with loose snow. I remember few climbs more agreeable than the ridge. Pitch by pitch we gladly unravelled its problems, which called for just enough sense and action to stimulate mind and body. We were led entrancedly upward. The Cogne valley lay behind; to our left glowing rock fell in jolting steps to an immaculate white glacier; to our right, still in shadow, were the glazed rocks, the ice and snow, of the north face. From the ridge, these last presented merely visual contrast, but all their condition implied was briefly brought home. Hoping to avoid an awkward tower we were lured from the warm crest. A short traverse on the shadowed face looked harmless enough, but we were soon scraping on glazed rock, searching in snow pockets for icy holds. With much time lost, we retreated to the ridge. Perhaps if the wispy clouds had not at this moment melted from our peak, revealing the final 300 feet (they had seemed the day's uncertainty) as no more formidable than the ground already made, we might have reflected on a warning. The message of the north face was not on our cheerful wave-length.

Noon found us at the summit, basking half-reclined on

a platform which held, and just held, the four of us. It was a situation and a mountain to give pleasure, a peak built with aesthetic care. Three rock ridges rose to achieve, where we relaxed, a perfect pyramid. Across a glittering foreground of snow, the ridges arrowed down to profound valley troughs. There in tides of green air one imagined birds and branches stirring and the hum of insects. Time passed. We knew we should be going, in a sense we wanted to go, but no one took the decision. Stirred at last from Olympian reverie, we stretched, dropped the detritus of luncheon in a crevice between the rocks, put on a rope, and considered our route. We could return, simply enough, the way we had come; to do so seemed mere repetition. We could take the accidented south ridge, not easy but in perfect condition; it would have landed us far from our base, involving a long glacier trudge late in the afternoon. The third ridge to the north-west was not in question; steepening monstrously in its lower section it led to a distant valley. There remained the ordinary and easy route off the peak. After briefly following this same north-west ridge, it struck back across an ice-slope, which normally carried a nap of sound snow, to a subsidiary rib. This in turn led comfortably to the valley below. But the existing conditions were far from normal and any descent on the north side of the mountain was an undertaking. Yet this was the route we chose, and chose unanimously. The choice was not thoughtless, for we all recalled the temper of the north face and our earlier excursion upon it, but as though made under compulsion. It seemed we were bound to take this route and no other; in this precise way the thread was spun.

As we worked down the first pitches of the north-west ridge on dry rock, the day still seemed pleasantly ours. A further error was yet to be made. Where we should have left the ridge, the snow-covered ice-slope swept smoothly down; across this slope, and some 400 feet below us, lay haven on the subsidiary rib. We tried the slope cautiously. Under pressure, the snow hesitated and then peeled off. Security lay in labour and the long cutting of ice-steps. But the ice was good and the security certain. We chose to disregard it, and once again the decision seemed imposed.

This was now our situation: immediately to the left lay the north-west ridge, soon steepening; at our feet the ice-slope; below and to the right the amiable rock-rib. However, far down the ice-slope, where the angle seemed momentarily to ease, a band of slabby rocks broke its smooth sweep. The rocks were uncomfortably placed, for beyond them the north face slithered over ice cliffs and disappeared from view. None the less we assumed an easy descent of the awkward north-west ridge to the level of the slabs, and then safe passage across them to the rock-rib beyond. In this light assumption I find again irrational compulsion. The mountains were watching.

The day, as I say, had been fine, giving no cause for suspicion. Now as we again moved down the north-west ridge, a wind began to blow, forcing up great bags of cloud to hide the sun. It pushed us off balance, worrying our feet like an angry dog, numbing our fingers, filling the rope with perverse life. At the same time, and suddenly between one pitch and another, the rocks became glazed. We were climbing on ice not granite. The change was as immediate, as forcibly emphasized, as the abrupt transitions of melodrama. The lights were darkened, the wind whistled, and there were the Sisters, spinning. The day was no longer ours. Yet involved in events we could hardly control, I recognized them as our own elaborate creation. Dry rock, a margin of time, a sensible route: we had decided to dispense with them all. This knife-like ridge of iced rock was but another of those predicaments to which an obstinate, yet seemingly conscious, blindness commits one. Here, built up as fatally as in everyday life, yet re-enacted in terms of cold and gravity, was the doomed sequence of events that leads to drink, the disastrous love affair, or madness. There was, there always is, something repugnant about the idiocy of such commitment, no doubt because it occurs so close to centres of dependable intelligence. It is a disfigurement that we carry like a tribal mark. 'This,' I thought, 'is the position into which human beings of their very nature will get themselves, and take pains to do so.'

In this altered fortune, there seemed initially no place for presence of mind. We climbed badly, holds were elusive, the day was wasting. It was late afternoon when we reached the band of slabs, with the ice cliffs falling away below. We had long and wearily recognized that the slabs would be glazed. They were also at a steeper angle than we had imagined, and very smooth. If the mountainside had been laid horizontal, they would have seemed like a school of glistening dolphins whose curved backs emerged from a glassy sea. At the point to which we had painfully descended that sea was bare ice, and the rocks themselves

68

were ice-filmed. A dangerously shallow sea, it nowhere offered the secure depth where we might lodge a piton. It was a traverse one would not willingly undertake, least of all in a tearing wind and late in the day.

We paused and the pause collected us, bringing a change of mood. There was now no alternative to the traverse. B. led it. Thirty years on mountains had left him with an accretion of knowledge, a technical carapace, that was as much a part of himself as arm or axe. It was instinctive, operating at a safer level than judgement and decision. Chipping nicks on the icy slabs, here and there something like a step in the thin couloirs, he moved deliberately out. The wind drowned all sound; we saw only the axe falling. Against the polished slope, finding toe-hold on the dolphin backs, was an isolated human figure in faded blue breeches, precariously yet somehow easily erect, apparently unaware that the ice rapids plunged to the darkening valley. As the rope ran out we followed one by one. B.'s footsteps became our own. Though I doubt if the passage was 300 yards, it seemed interminable, but it was now simply a matter of moving with care, of applying technique. There was no scope for the faulty sunlit decisions which had earlier misled us. We had realized in time that the mountains were watching. We reached the rib as dusk fell. 'No further problems,' my diary reads, and masks my feelings. Yet I know, that there (as on the Pic d'Oo) I received an insight into that curious voluntary blindness which at every altitude is wrongly called Fate.

*   *   *

Our pleasure lay much in being alone. From a morning

when we left village and valley to an afternoon, three or four days later, when mule and muleteer would return to fetch us, we saw no one. It was our own country, even as it had been Packe's and Russell's. Though the world grew every day more crowded, the Spanish Pyrenees had never offered greater solitude. The Civil War and the second World War had brought a temporary traffic of flight and conspiracy. This was at an end. Meanwhile 'progress' had, surprisingly, raised the mountain barrier ever higher between the last village in each French valley and the first village on the Spanish side. The mule tracks over the passes, which for centuries had carried a commerce, often contraband, were deserted. In places they were hardly visible, retaining definition only in the steeper zig-zags which had once been laboriously paved and cobbled. It was now cheaper to provide a lorry with a false bottom and detour goods a hundred miles by metalled road. As for the generality of climbers, they had abandoned the Pyrenees decades earlier. Knowing usually the French slopes with their abominable rock, to which honourable exceptions are few, they had removed to the firmer ridges and the greater challenge of the Alps. In this year, indeed in three summers in the Spanish Pyrenees, we saw only one climbing party. On the confines of the Pole the sight could hardly have surprised us more. Through our glasses we viewed the specks on a distant snow-slope, and moved in the opposite direction.

Yet in this deserted country we sometimes had companionship of another sort. There were days when we both accepted the sense of a third person climbing with us, and in the setting it seemed normal. Suddenly he was there: a stone dislodged by his invisible boot tinkled down the hillside; his invisible mouth made inroad on our provisions; and behind me I would catch the flavour, but not the sense, of some murmured phrase, or, casting about for a route, accept inaudible suggestions not always well-considered. As suddenly we would be again alone, and speaking relapse into the intimacy of a conversation that is only for two. This third presence is often reported by mountaineers, and I suppose was summoned by the suggestible abstraction into which we fell plodding across long slopes. Yet I have never known it so palpable as in these weeks, and for a time I fancied Don Miguel there. But the presence was too untroubled. Relaxed and reassuring, it came for its pleasure, and I think enjoyed the country and the exercise.

Our wandering had something of the idyllic and the pastoral. With our contented camps set in the borderland between abundance below and the bareness above, we knew no reason to shift them but such as we ourselves suggested: curiosity for a fresh valley, or the impulsion towards a peak whose very shape was unknown to us, a name on a map that was growing tattered. We were not pressed, and we held time haltered. In a century that abjectly observes its sad divisions, that lives by appointments and by diaries (where ironically survive in small italics the half-forgotten seasonal feasts, equinox and solstice), time's only discipline, willingly assumed, was the span of a day: the shadowy start, the climb, and the return to camp at evening.

The residual memory of these days, the ambergris that

scents them, includes the simplest and most reliable of mountain pleasures. In a cosseted existence we have no urgent wants. It is true that a woman will sometimes elude us, but our desire for food, for warmth, for rest, for sleep, is never imperative. The only shrill calls in our curtained rooms are the time signals from our diaries. Conscience not hunger keeps the lunch appointment, and only boredom drives us from the party to our beds. In the mountains at the end of most days one is tired and one's stomach is empty. One longs for food and sleep. Even the cessation of movement is a goal. And regularly these things were given us, fully, completely. Hungry and tired we ate and rested, and in the middle of a sentence fell asleep. These were not small rewards.

There were other days, and they can always be relied on in the mountains, with nothing, absolutely nothing, to do. Such days linked the present and the past. As through the open tent-flap I watched the curl and drift of snow-flakes, my mind would come to rest on time past as naturally as the snow on the ground. In my complete inactivity, fragments of time would then effortlessly present themselves in upper Aragon at 6000 feet: the face of a friend who died of measles at school, the sensation of thrusting on a bicycle fast into the twilight, my home by the Seine, the Dog's Mercury that unaccountably covered the islands overnight in spring, and other memories of later date presented with no better logic. Events I had thought forgotten would heliograph desperately from the setting sun of a distant afternoon and find rescue. As stones under water are brighter, so these events as I saw them through time appeared more real than in their first enactment. The faces and feelings that emerged into the flickering light of snow gave another dimension to these inactive days and suggested, as the mountains seemed sometimes to suggest, that my lengthening life might possess a significance as yet unexplained.

*   *   *

When provisions ran out, we went to the Spanish villages that stood at the valley-heads and turned their backs resolutely on the mountains. Clustered stone cells, rising from spare rocky soils, they looked like embrowned honeycombs. Yet for all their appearance of organic growth, they had architectural dignity in the receding roof-planes disposed one above another up a hillside, in the simple loggias cutting sun and shadow into solid chunks, and in the plainly moulded entries, hung with enormous doors, that led to courtyards. The only elaboration was the village church with its arcaded tower. Built in the decades of heady enthusiasm which followed the expulsion of the Muslims, it had fortunately undergone little change, unless it were in the furious Civil War. The villages never straggled, and the low-roofed houses pressing together in a common purpose concealed their inner life. As we approached, unglazed windows lent them a blind look. No one seemed to be moving. Voices, if heard at all, rose beyond intervening walls. The crazy alleys gave little away. Life was in courtyards, in stables, in small twilit shops beyond black rectangles of open doorway. It was oriental in its withdrawn quality and one penetrated with

73

difficulty to the cellular activity of the honeycomb people. The contrast with the open mountains was agreeable.

These were prosperous villages as things go in Spain, and there were no landlords but the villagers themselves. Their holdings here in upper Aragon were large enough to support a family and, unlike those of the Galician peasants, had not been sub-divided to scraps of unworkable ground. Perhaps because of this relative well-being, the people were conservative. We heard them arguing bitterly of civil strife and found their theme was the old Carlist quarrel. The area had been a Carlist stronghold. Dignified and self-sufficient, yet not unfriendly, they had been little corrupted by strangers. While at the barber's in such a village, and one of the larger, I saw a crowd collect outside his open door. While he was removing my seven days' beard, word had got about that I was English. Emissaries came for confirmation, and murmured inquiry went on above my head. They were unconvinced. They had not heard of the Costa Brava and the news seemed improbable. When I emerged a village elder formally addressed me: 'Are you, Sir, an Englishman? We wish, with respect, to know, since we have never seen one.' I was pleased that this could happen only 200 kilometres from Biarritz as crows fly. So it seemed were they. With the elder and other persons I discussed the matter further over a bottle of wine at the *fonda*.

Benasque was the largest and certainly the most distinguished of these villages. In time past, before seaside resorts were fashionable or mammoth hotels rose at San Sebastian, the Aragonese nobility removed to Benasque in summer to escape the heat of the plains. Their houses, mainly of the seventeenth and eighteenth centuries, the palaces of the Count of Ribagorza and the Baron of Benasque, were now ruinous or more humbly employed, but they gave the village a flavour of unconscious grandeur. Though mules were tethered to mullioned windows, and weeds sprouted from delicate string-courses, the carved classical detail was still sharp above the alleys. Doorways carried the elaborate escutcheons of families who had spent their last summer season in Benasque before the Peninsular War. Through such doorways, pushing aside the bead curtains that kept out the air but not the flies, we went to replenish our stores. Though there was little choice, it always took time. There was no sense of urgency in Benasque. At the wine shop, the last and most essential point of call, we had to drink a few glasses while we discussed how best to fill our twin wicker-covered demi-johns. Pleasant but idle discussion: it was always the same crude brandy and coarse red wine. The demijohns, balanced comfortably on either side of the mule, seemed to promise a succession of agreeable evenings beside our fire. It was odd how quickly the jars emptied. It may have been the chilly nights needed warming, or the mugs were large, or perhaps the nature of the drink. This was no brandy to linger over.

Belloc, to whom one must often defer in the Spanish Pyrenees, would have approved our liberal supply of wine. We could not approve his advocacy of the *botta*, the leathern bottle of the people. Its furry goatskin stomach never ceases to stink, and one wastes much liquor in trying to sweeten it. Nor could we echo his praise of *alpagates*, the local rope-soled shoes. But, even as we encumbered ourselves with provisions in the dusky sharp-smelling interiors of Benasque, we admired his stern fashion of travel, his spare fare. He was the eloquent expert of this region, and we repeatedly bowed to the truth of his observations.

The choice of provisions reveals, often with little flattery, the idiosyncrasies of mountaineers. Precisely because so deep an expression of personality, it is an explosive matter. When every ounce counts, people will fall out over dried apricots or raspberry jam. Preferences hardly conscious at the dinner-table become imperative. A gulf appears between 'sour' and 'sweet' men. An insistence on smoked cheese will unbalance the packs and temper of an expedition. Personal gear is of course one's own affair. Yet again what differences are revealed, and what penetrating conclusions can be drawn. Though frugal enough in other matters, I always take too many gloves: silk undergloves, homely mittens, leather gauntlets, and enormous waterproof affairs for blizzards (like crazy top-boots for hands); and regularly most of them come back in the bottom of my rucksack undisturbed. Hardly more disturbed are the books I take. I should know by now that mountains call for easy reading, and jealously admit only Wilkie Collins or brief poems that can be swallowed in a minute. Herrick serves. Yet one never learns. The *Anatomy of Melancholy* is lugged for weeks over peaks and passes to return unopened. Experience shows that in bad weather a pocket chess-set is more to the purpose. Above all, it is unwise to take books about mountaineering. Their quality is one of the puzzles of literature. Whymper wrote well, but few mountaineers have done so. The puzzle is the more baffling when one recalls all the good books about the desert. Mountain and desert inspire the same compulsive devotion, and their beauty, for those who know them, is of a wholly different order from that of other landscape; yet, while almost no Englishman has written badly of Arabia, mountaineers in print rarely do justice to themselves or the dignity of their subject. The white dunes of the Alps, flowing majestically as those of Negd, and the great peaks, compelling as the distances of the Empty Quarter, have too often been celebrated in terms narrowly technical or broadly facetious. Mountain literature is not for the rucksack.

It would be late afternoon before we escaped from Benasque to plod, with heavily-laden mule, into the hills. There was a point where one stopped and looked back (those drinks in the wine shop had made a pause welcome) to find that the village had contracted, had again drawn in upon itself. The roofs touched, overlapped; there were no longer separate houses, or alleys, or shops, or people, only the honeycomb, the brown wart on the thread of the Esera. We felt a momentary loneliness. Sometimes we weakened and stayed the night. The heart of Benasque was the Fonda del Sayo, kept by the Abadias family. They were hunters, fishermen, and in their own way mountaineers. The iron cross we had seen on the Pont de Mahomet marked the spot where an Abadias had been killed by lightning. Antonio, the patriarch, was resolute, voluble and friendly, and made his inn like home. In the upstairs lavatory, which sensibly enough no one used, there was a

77

bees' nest. The wall dripped with honey, and one woke in the adjoining room to a murmur, as though lying in a field of clover at midday. The general room below gave directly on the kitchen. It was shadowy, perhaps merely by contrast with the hot sun outside and the bars of sunlight which filtered through the shutters. In a corner, the most obscure, four men played cards, always; and always the same men. Though the bottle of wine was recharged, they never broke off their deep game to eat. Sometimes one might catch them absently swallowing an olive off a little plate. Whether it were ten in the morning or ten at night, the timeless game was in progress, sometimes in silence but for the slap of cards on the table, sometimes the voices raised, all speaking together, to die away unaccountably. The low-ceilinged room itself was timeless; only the slats of hot light moved on the floor, slipped from the edges of the wooden tables, and disappeared at evening. There were no set hours for meals. One could order dinner, and cause no surprise, at any moment between noon and midnight. We came to count on stuffed olives, grilled trout, and a liquorish purée of pears. The trout were unfailing, fresh and very small, from the raging waters of the Esera. José, the son of the house, took them expertly on a spinner, a hundred yards away, a fish at every other cast.

Drinking anis in this shadowy room, listening to the slapping cards, and dreaming of trout after a long walk down the valley, we were handed a note, though how it came to find us at Benasque was a mystery. On the twist of discoloured paper that Antonio Abadias brought from the kitchen, Don Miguel had written majestically and briefly: 'I am at the Baths of Bohi.' It was a summons. Of Caldas de Bohi we knew two things: that it was the point of entry to wild and attractive mountains, a group which comprised the Aiguilles de Travesany whose fretted outline imagination had already drawn for us; and that it was perilously close to the Encantados. From Caldas they could be reached in a day's walk by the Plateau of the Shepherds, and the harmless *portarron*, or Little Pass, of Espot. Late that night opening our bedroom window we heard the river roaring and grumbling, inordinately loud, through the sleeping village. Far or near the sound of the Esera or its tributaries had for days been with us. From our window we could see dark shapes ranged round its watershed, and we thought affectionately of the camping grounds that we were now ordered to abandon. Next morning for the last time we were woken by the bees. They were in stinging mood.

Though only some twenty-five kilometres across intervening ridges, Caldas de Bohi was three times the distance by road. We got there in a motor-car, dusty and jolted, towards evening. For centuries the sick journeyed to Bohi for the waters; the poor swaying up the remote valley on horse or mule; the rich couched on palanquins. The sombre stone buildings held hope, and some presumably returned to the plains cured by the waters. The approach had not much changed. Though the mule track had become a dirt road, boulders from the steep hillsides still bombarded it after rain, and at the head of the valley, removed from the heat, the dust, and the utilitarian buildings, lay snow-shoulders and rock summits.

It is necessary to insist on this background—the cistus and juniper, the shale, the cold piping cry of the goat-herd, the rushing streams, the snow and the peaks above—if one is to convey the nastiness of Caldas de Bohi. The abrupt meeting of man and nature calls for tact. None was exercised here. The road ended at the Baths, and in a first moment of innocence we looked with interest at the mediaeval buildings. The swimming pool was screened by trees and the whirl of the snow water drowned the blare of the radio. Though we should have been warned by the petrol pump, always an ominous sign, and the parked cars winking in the afternoon sun, the horrid transformation was not immediately apparent. Only turning a corner did we meet the striped umbrellas, the tables ankle-deep in yellow gravel, and the canned music that surged from a chromium bar. At the tables sat white, faintly moustached women in tight black silk, and men, as darkly dressed, turning newspapers. They perspired quietly in the sinking sun. It was impossible to guess whom they might be: rich undertakers from Zaragosa, bank managers from Huesca and Jaca, widows and widowers from Seo d'Urguel? No doubt as innocent and sad as the visitors to most spas, they were in these mountains painfully out of place.

There was no sign of Don Miguel. He had left two days previously, and his departure had been welcomed by the management and the guests. It appeared that he had been quietly insolent and continually drunk. Of our horrible evening there is little to say. The beer from the flashing refrigerator was warm, and when in foolish desperation we tried to revive our spirits with martinis they were pale brown. There were no bees in our tiled lavatory, and it did not smell of honey. The cold tap ran scalding. In the vast dining-room, where a five-course dinner dragged its taste-less length, we were silenced by insistent music. There was no release but sleep. Mule and muleteer would not be with us until morning.

All horrors end; at ten next day we were loaded and off to the mountains. I have three times climbed to the upper valley of the Rio Malo, and each time have arrived elated by effects of landscape elaborate yet utterly natural, by a sequence of impressions that led to a perfect conclusion. At first the mule track mounted—and how one's spirits mounted too as the isolated spa shrank in the valley below —over troubled ground. This was once the tumbled detritus below the snout of an ancient glacier, but time had rooted pines and alders in crevices, had covered boulders with moss and couched them on grass. A green unguent had spread over the wounds and sealed the slope. As we topped its crest, the Lago de los Caballeros lay before us in unruffled contrast. The lake, whose name speaks of vanished horsemen, is the *adagio* passage. The mountains that rise abruptly on either side, leaning back on the sky, have no part in it. They accentuate the gathered quality of the calm. As we skirted the lawn-like fringes of the water, the ground, like an expensive ballroom, seemed sprung beneath our feet. At the lake's end a steep slope, like a giant talus, down which a branch of the Rio Malo forced angry passage, rose 1,500 feet. The slope was pale grey and green, for bedded in the turf were enormous bone-like polished shapes, scoured by the lost glacier, perhaps the finest *roches moutonnées* in Europe. With the heaving mule clattering in jerks and rushes up one of those stone-paved Pyrenean tracks that are now deserted, we reached the top in a hot noon. Our heads seemed to touch the sky, and all was before us, palpable and perfect, to be inhaled with a long amazed breath.

As though cupped in two vast hands, an ample saucer rested below a crescent of snow-mottled peaks. To one side rose the Aiguilles to Travesany with their dramatic sky-line; to the other rose the Pic del Mig and the Beciberri; facing us at a dignified distance was the shapely Montarto. Here was the prototype of all gentle upland valleys. The saucer held a series of lakes, revealed progressively as we walked. They were separated by rock-shapes, smooth as basking hippopotami, and by intimate useless pastures. From these improbable isthmuses and curiously-shaped territories, the snow had only recently withdrawn. We set our camp above the Lago Negre, beside whose inlets grew a few twisted pines, the only trees in our landscape. Towards evening the trout began to rise: a single thin circle like a prick on the still water, then another and another, as though from a clear sky the whole lake were pocked with rain drops. These were the trout that our muleteer pursued relentlessly. Coming back from a day's climbing we would find a row of them laid in order of size, firm and luscious on the grass.

From our tent the peaks were two to three thousand feet above, as though placed to offer the perfect day for a middle-aged mountaineer. For rock there was nothing to match the Aiguilles de Travesany. In a warm windless air, we traversed the serrated ridge and found solid granite. The successive crests, each a little higher than the last, led delightfully to the summit. Sulphur anemones and the large blue gentian shared the ledges where we placed our belays. An ancient rope sling, set for a *rappel* above an awkward passage, proved we had our predecessors. They had been discreet. This length of rope and a couple of pegs were their only tokens on all our Spanish climbs. As we rose higher, the geography of the outspread saucer became explicit. The lakes which had seemed to lie haphazard behind each fold of ground and outcrop of rock acquired their logic: we saw the threads of silver that linked them and the orderly sequence that gathered all these waters and finally flung them down the polished talus to the Lago de los Caballeros.

As the day wore on, our ridge threw its black shadow eastward, and where it fell on a chaos of boulders our climb was mimicked by shadow-shapes, our second selves. We were very small. Returning to camp we watched white towers building in the sky, battlemented cumuli climbing to dizzy heights. The crazy constructions circled uneasily over the mountains. As the summer storm built up, the clouds tortured with electricity began to strain, boil, and mutter. A first violent thunderclap struck our saucer like a blow and echoed from peak to peak. It was the prelude to a barrage. Soon blast and echo were indistinguishable and intermingled, allowing no moment of silence. The storm was the more formidable because no ripple of air reached us from the savage concussions above. The few raindrops that fell were like enormous tears, each one a distinct slap on rock or turf. We waited awed for the storm that never broke. At last the preoccupied monsters moved away grappling, and the battle diminished to a distant rumble. We judged that they spent themselves eastward on the Encantados, pounding and sluicing those bare peaks in an orgasm of rage. A clear sky succeeded, and moonlight later filled our saucer and glistened on the Lago Negre. Standing outside the tent before going to sleep, I noticed it shining on our axe-heads. Concentrating the light, the steel seemed to burn, yet conveyed utter tranquillity.

The upper valley of the Rio Malo remains rich in occasions. There is the morning, approaching the Pic del Mig, when we floundered in a drift of the rare white lily, *Liliastrum Bertolina*; the return from the Beciberri, when I discovered, only 200 feet below an austere snow-field, a hot sunny gorge where the diffused spray of a waterfall fell like constant dew and nurtured within its damp circle a tropical growth of peony, orchid, and rhododendron. Drops of clear water gathered on fronds and velvet petals, formed minute transparent lakes in brilliant calices, or slid down pulpy stems to a saturated earth. Different in its impact, yet as memorable, was a certain iced lake below the Punta Harlé. One of the sombre *estanys glacats*, so characteristic of the central Pyrenees, it bore no relationship to the friendly waters of the saucer but was no less beautiful. It lay beneath a semi-circle of cliffs; above these sloped the steep snow-field that fed the lake throughout the summer and supplied the bergs which floated there motionless. The lake was held in a rocky cup, and as the snows melted the excess of water lapped away silently over the rim. The lake was deep, and its depth was marked by shades of blue that towards the centre grew black. No scrap of vegetation found a hold among the rocks. Even the choughs kept away. As one approached, a noticeable drop in the air temperature raised the flesh on one's arms. The sun reached it for an hour or two, and the wind rarely. (As I have said, the floating mounds of snow were motionless.) On the brightest day with the snow gleaming on the slopes above the cliffs, the lake was sombre. It also seemed merciless, for nothing could live in that water. Changeless and icy it was the negation of life, a profound yet valuable contrast to the invitations of the idyllic valley.

*   *   *

We were not always alone in the upper Rio Malo. John joined us, and Myles. The latter, accredited as our botanist, was large and handsome, attributes that seemed inappropriate to a reflective and subtle temper. For one having no Spanish, his impact on young Spaniards was remarkable. From villages disgustingly wrapped in the afternoon siesta, he would conjure muleteers to compete for our employ. Peasants for him would walk kilometres to fetch provisions or guide us to a ford. In his botanical capacity he was idle. His collecting was done in a silk dressing-gown on the green fringes of pellucid lakes, and in the temperate hours when the sun was high yet not insistent. By noon, botany abandoned, he had taken to the water. Later, stretched on warm rocks, he slept or studied the skies of upper Aragon. Hating snow, he declined our packed and scrambling days. On our return, we would see him from afar combing his xanthic locks beside some inviting stretch of water where, it may be presumed, no one else had ever bathed. I began to feel that motionless he had come closer to the heart of the Rio Malo than we in our activity. John, a painter as will appear, was remarkable for many things, among them a determination at all times to make true distinctions and think nothing of the achievement. Unfortunately, for this was to have sad consequences, his virtues were closely compounded with courtesy. In other years there were to be other friends, and above all Basil, the perfect companion in such mountains.

One morning I woke to realize that time was running short. If the Encantados were to be climbed, there was no day to lose. Less than twenty-four hours later and intolerably early, John and I, an advance party, left the sleeping camp and set off for the Lake of San Mauricio that lies snug at the feet of the Encantados. The way led through country as engaging and as apparently empty as all this region. We had been going several hours when from a pass we first saw our smooth grey peaks. Rising from an entrenched valley, they carried wisps of snow and their clean shapes dominated the dark mirror of San Mauricio as well as imagination could have wished. The valley itself was greener and more relaxed, the struggling pines more numerous, than is usual in these Spanish mountains. On the flank of the valley where we hurried down, it was almost woodland. In places the noon sun was totally excluded or laid, between spreading evergreens, white patterns as arbitrary as the pieces of a jig-saw puzzle. We

passed and re-passed from sun to shade, ourselves altern-
ately bright and dark. The shade as we stepped into it was
opaque as a curtain, the obscurity a repeated surprise that
left us stumbling. Yet before we emerged our sight was
each time sharpened; looking from shadow we saw the
next wedge of sunlight streaked with floating filaments and
dusted with insect wings. Wading through these pools of
light, we seemed with each breath to sip the plankton of
warm yellow seas. This coloured water bore no resem-
blance to the clear draughts we had drunk in the early
morning. Everything here was different, for we were in
the drugged aura of the Encantados.

It was from a drapery of shadow that the two hairy
brigands rose to seize us, waving their guns like hockey
sticks. When one had slapped me gently (no doubt I was
over-excited), we resigned ourselves to capture. Shouting
their brigand nonsense, and flourishing their atrocious
guns, they lugged us up the hillside. We had no eye now
for filaments and wings, though there must have been
plenty in the cruel clearing where their tents were pitched.
I noticed in a dazed way that iron implements were being
heated over a crackling fire and recalled that abominations
were said still to be practised in the region. I also remember
a momentary feeling of surprise on noting that these wild
fellows had dug a latrine. It seemed a strange concession
to another order of ideas. We were soon admitted to the
presence of their leader. Before a splendid view, he was
seated on a camp stool in a bay of sunlight among the
trees, and he was painting. As he ignored us and our
persecutors, I had time to observe that on his canvas the

sun was setting over the Encantados, not its customary point of decline, and certainly with effects that seemed exaggerated. His appearance recalled Adolphe Menjou in his earlier films, and it fitted the part that he should have been dressed (loot no doubt) in black riding boots and the close-fitting uniform of a Spanish officer. The calf of his right boot where he had been wiping his hog's hair brush was a gay mosaic of colour.

When at last, with his brush poised like a dart, he looked us up and down, his manner, languid and distant, seemed closely modelled on the great actor. The decadent Hadji-Stavros, I surmised, of twentieth-century Aragon, and remorseless. 'Passports,' he said to our surprise, and looked with a final satisfied glance at his canvas. Rummaging in our rucksacks, we produced them with relief. Light had dawned; these must be the frontier guards of whom we had heard. He accepted the trim blue documents with little enthusiasm. They seemed in such a setting but feeble recommendation. Having looked at mine and coldly returned it, he opened John's. The start, the stare, which ensued were the beginning of our misfortune. He turned on his camp stool to face us, rose, and carefully straightened his uniform. 'Sir,' he said to John, 'you are a painter?' 'Yes indeed,' replied John with the empty smile that we reserve for customs officers and persons in authority. Menjou bowed formally and extended a fine paint-stained hand. 'I too,' he said, indicating with a possessive yet modest air two square feet of sunset.

In the *détente* that followed our ruffians were swept away with a gesture. We seemed almost free men when John, with the natural courtesy that was to serve us so ill, turned to the canvas. He overlooked no hint of merit in that pedestrian work. The growling shadows in the valley, the rioting colour in the sky, the toppling cliffs of the Encantados, all came in for their appreciation. Before I knew it he had dropped the name of Turner, and soon we were swopping the Masters, with delicate emphasis on the Spanish School. Brandy and glasses arrived, with two more chairs. Menjou's interest in every aspect of art-history was, if not profound, insatiable. Among his tattered men he lacked instructed company, and here were we, a gift from heaven. In the circumstances we were ignobly ready with those shared allusions, those easy deviations from one name to another, that extend talk on a common theme. The communion was all too complete. Yet John did better than I. It was not simply that he knew more, but that Menjou's evident plight, his near-starvation, his cultural rickets, made an immediate appeal. Faced with a fellow-being in extreme deprivation, he could only and nobly respond. I was soon out of the running, and turned my attention to the brandy. It smelt of violets, a phenomenon unfamiliar to connoisseurs of *fine* but not unusual in upper Aragon. By the time a ruffian, the same who had dealt so lightly with me earlier, appeared with an ingratiating leer and a second bottle, even John was showing signs of exhaustion. There could be few more Spanish masters in reserve, and the shadows were lengthening. If we were to attempt the Encantados next day, escape was imperative. But Menjou was still fresh and the scent good. With a hospitable wave at the violets, he got back to his subject. We

89

were his prisoners. I recalled that in not dissimilar circumstances one of Mr Waugh's characters had read Dickens aloud for *years* on a tributary of the Amazon.

In due course a table appeared in our bay of fading sunlight. Upon it bottles of red wine were as liberally placed as chessmen. There we were gorged like reluctant geese, every mouthful substantiating our artistic communion, every bottle making the Encantados more inaccessible. We had reached the goat's cheese, and the thing seemed to be drawing to its hysterical end, when John, no doubt dazed, reverted to an unfortunate topic we had left when the day was younger: the works of Menjou. It was an opening that our companion, by now our close friend, would never miss. We must see his paintings. They would enable us to obtain, for subsequent report in Paris and London, a just notion of his powers. John summoned an expectant smile and, with resistance weakened by violets and chessmen, I hiccoughed assent. Despairing so long, I had now ceased to care. Soon from the embowering trees the first canvas emerged, formally presented between two desperadoes. It was another sunset; many were to follow. Steadily, yet how deliberately, the canvases came and went. The supply of attendant man-power was inexhaustible, and we sat like some powerless hanging-committee whose thumbs could never be turned down. Words soon failed us. We could only nod and mime, raising a hand as though the magnificence of the thirtieth view of the Encantados (*my* Encantados, I sourly thought) had robbed us of speech. Such tribute was enough for Menjou; I have rarely seen a happier man. Between canvases we drank shaky toasts. By the time the last work was presented, we sat in twilight. Though I do not believe the uncharitable thought crossed John's mind, I realized with pleasure that our host's qualities, at least as a military man, must be totally unappreciated in Madrid; he had spent years exiled on his camp stool. If Menjou were ever summoned to greater responsibility, a train of mules would hardly carry his sunsets away.

Sunsets exploding in our heads, we woke late next morning. For some time we sat listlessly, looking out between the trees. There were the Encantados; there, clearly visible, a route up the north face. The mountain in perfect condition might have been ours that morning. But now, past noon, the weather was breaking. When we turned sadly homeward for the Rio Malo, clouds were pressing on the summit. Menjou was still asleep, but a picturesque escort accompanied us to the pass. It only put ironic edge on our failure. Soon the rain came down, steady, unconcerned, universal. We dripped and squelched. By the time we reached camp, late, tired and dispirited though bringing (R. said) an aroma of violets, the water had long since penetrated our anoraks, and runnels had found their way to our very crutches.

For two days rain drummed on the tent. There was food but, as R. calmly announced, no bread. On our elbows, in cramped attitudes, we learnt to eat marmalade with sardines *nature*. We got warm at intervals by lighting a Primus stove, which in the confinement of the tent roared like a tiger. Myles managed to sleep most of the time and showed the weather no resentment. John, I hoped, was reflecting on the drawback of good manners and the penalty of being a painter. Personally I could only think of the Encantados, lost in the storm-bound end of our summer, and question why, time and again, we had thrown away in wandering pleasure the very thing we had come for. It seemed a calculated misjudgement. Staring gloomily through the tent flap, I saw grey veils draw endlessly across the upland saucer, and heard everywhere the rustle and splash of running water. Below us the Lago Negre was angry and black as its name. The mountains above, seen through the intervening rain as through a mist, were white with new snow.

We broke camp on the third day as soon as it was light. It still rained and the tent had been leaking for twenty-four hours. Our descent to Bohi was a rout. The mule track down the long glacis to the Lago de los Caballeros had become a frothing torrent, through which we and our beast stumbled and staggered. The crossing of the Rio Malo, furious and dangerously swollen, was barely achieved. A bedraggled and silent party reached the Baths. In such circumstances they seemed a haven. The umbrellas were furled, the pebbly patio was deserted, but at the chromium-plated bar a solitary black figure sat twirling a glass. 'I have been waiting for you,' remarked Don Miguel. His tone was that of a commander whose picked troops have let him down. He knew that the Encantados had escaped us. As we talked with enthusiasm of our other climbs and mountains, he looked disillusioned.

In the afternoon, with the rain clouds drawing away, R., Don Miguel and I drove up the Noguera Pallaresa, bound for the Val d'Aran and France. At the head of the Noguera valley we stopped at the primitive hospice. Here mule traffic had always halted before climbing the track, defined in worn zig-zags, up and over the steep mountain flank. Probably the track would never be used again, for the new road by which we had come disappeared into the sore mouth of a tunnel that was to link this remote valley with the north. In the hospice a wood fire burned in the centre of the largest room, on a floor flagged with enormous stones, and the smoke in ancient fashion found its way out by a funnel and louvre through the roof. The room smelt of pine, for the funnel was deeply encrusted with the slimy resinous deposits of the wood fires of centuries. Here we had a last melancholy drink, and left Don Miguel to unspecified business. As we parted, he said, 'Next year come to me at Salardu . . . for the Encantados.' It was the only reference he made to our failure.

The tunnel was not yet officially open, but Don Miguel had arranged things. About its mouth lay the usual signature of progress: shacks, empty oil drums, bags of concrete, twisted rusting metal. Its length, dimly lit by naked bulbs strung on loops of wire, was a raw desolation. Lacerated rock protruded from the unmetalled surface. Water dripped from the ceiling and the walls, and we jolted slowly from puddle to puddle. Our course, alone in the bowels of a tortured mountain, had the quality of nightmare. But we were not altogether alone. Heads down, hooves splashing through the water, moving steadily as on a mountainside, a flock of sheep came towards us. As they passed unconcernedly, we stopped and switched off the engine, only to hear echoing down the tunnel the high-pitched cry of their shepherd, recalling the hill pastures of all Mediterranean countries. It sounded like a knell. If we were to return with pleasure to the Encantados, it must be soon or not at all.

III

THE MOUNTAIN

In the following June we drove again up the Val d'Aran and found Lès awake, for it was only the eve of the feast. The valley, more suave and pastoral than I remembered it, seemed to welcome this return. The first crop of hay had been taken from the meadows along the river and they looked smooth as lawns. The winding band of green contrasted with the scrawny hillsides, already searing in the midsummer sun. Like veins, the green here and there penetrated the lateral valleys, twisting deep into the hills. At the valley heads snow-blotched peaks appeared, remote and benign. There was a freshness in the day with its first taste of mountain air, and the life of the villages perched above the road, those stone honeycombs crowned with bell-towers, seemed enviable.

When we asked for Don Miguel at Salardu he was away, 'probably at the inn over the pass'. Beyond Salardu the green ribbon shrank. The meadows, though still delightfully shorn and smooth, became defensive enclaves threatened by scrub and boulder. The screens of poplar and ragged oak which had divided one pasture from another disappeared. Where the road began to wind decisively in laced bends to the pass, junipers and scattered pines succeeded and enormous patches of broom spilled like yellow landslides down the slopes. Though closed by snow for six months of the year, the Col de Bonaigüe, bridging the curious fault that separates the western and eastern halves of the range, is one of the least forbidding of Pyrenean passes. It was smooth as velvet, an expanse of turf in whose hollows lay stranded whales of snow. On either side itsun dulations stretched to the mountain flanks, but the peaks were distant enough to leave a sense of bright space. A breeze, dying away from time to time, drifted over the short grass.

As we sat there, we recalled the tunnel, for another flock of sheep, as though to reassure us, appeared from the dead ground below our vision. They were the first of the summer migrations from sere valleys to the richer pastures of the Val d'Aran and the north. They lapped, perhaps 2,000 of them, in a wave up the slope, hesitating yet pressing forward like foam up a beach. The consignment probably of several villages, they bore the brands of many owners. It was an immemorial movement and the crooks that the hired shepherds held must have been among the oldest implements in the world. The men brought nothing for their long stay but a blanket slung over one shoulder, a wine-filled *botta*, a woollen bag with food, and their restless dogs. Preceded by one or two wise goats, as is the southern custom, the sheep flowed and rippled towards us. Suddenly we were among them, drowned in fleece. As suddenly they were past. For a moment longer we saw them, their pace quickened to that of a torrent, pouring and jostling into the Val d'Aran. We long heard the bells of the old ewes and the cries of the shepherds. With their passing, the sunny place became empty. We looked at the mountains, radiant but with a precise note of cold; we sensed the winds that swept the Col de Bonaigüe in winter and the driving snows that buried it.

The Val d'Aran is almost an Alpine valley. The contrast where we looked towards the Noguera Pallaresa spoke unmistakably of Spain. Here was a bony, resilient landscape, and a few dark pines merely accentuated the new range of colour, verdigris, red, and yellow. The inn lay below the pass, yet well above the steep decline where the yet insignificant waters of the Noguera plunge southward among rocks and tangled alders. Primitive, low, embrowned, its stone walls had sheltered travellers for centuries. It was of great age and a place to which people came in need. Its only advertisement was a faded board that read *Sanctuario de Nuestra Senhora de Los Ares*.

We found Don Miguel absorbed in an old newspaper. He wore the same black suit and his glass was beside him on the table. He had probably cadged a lift from the valley, avidly greeting the peaks at each turn in the road. For all the surprise he showed, he might have been awaiting us. Perhaps he was. A twitch at the smoke-stained corner of a lip may have indicated the importance of our return. Our own attachment to the mountains seemed superficial. When he had called for drinks, it became clear that our plans were already laid and our course set. We were not to muff the Encantados twice. In the previous year he had sent us off, not unwilling, to the Aneto; we had overstayed. This time we were to conduct our preliminary climbing from his own valley and almost beneath his eye. Then, like sensible people, we were to take the best, the logical, route

99

to the Encantados, down the Noguera Pallaresa and up the lateral valley that climbs steeply to the village of Espot, only a mile or two from our objective. Perhaps consciously, we had disregarded this approach in the previous summer, obscurely preferring a wilder introduction from the west. At Espot we were promised a good inn. 'Whisky,' said Don Miguel. Our hearts sank, for in the Pyrenees this ally keeps company with progress and things undesirable.

Lorry-drivers and muleteers drifted in, breaking their journey over the pass to spend the eve of St John. With the lamps came an air of festivity and the rap of glasses. Looking about me, I recalled that a Spaniard, wearied by an Englishwoman's talk of the shortcomings of Spanish government, had answered, 'Yes, Madam, but have you noticed that all my countrymen have *faces*.' From the noise and the smell of cheap wine that soon filled the room, Don Miguel withdrew from time to time for those private conversations which his business demanded. Once he rejoined us with a bundle of skins, blandly announcing that they had been obtained before the ban on the hunting of the izard. The ban was many years old. Later he brought to our corner an acquaintance. The man had come from a *feria* in the plains and taken several mule-days on the journey. Recollection held him. He evoked again and again the name of a glistening bull-fighter, as a man might call on a saint. His talk in the low room lit up the arid peninsula. He still heard the savage clanging of church bells and the gaudy boys beating drums; he saw the sculptured capes and bulls sinking to their knees, the coloured lights and the sweaty dancing in streets where the noise was greater at midnight than at noon. For another year he would carry on mountain tracks, like an echo, this clamour of a white-hot town.

In the adjoining kitchen blackened pots were slung over a wood fire. In a reek of garlic, with hay-forks and mole traps hanging on the wall, we ate slabs of home-smoked ham, mutton grilled over the logs, and a mess of mushrooms. We swilled it down with a red wine that burnt the tongue. Their night was barely started when we took our candles to bed. Waking, I heard hours later the men singing (shades of Belloc), yet even as I tried to catch the words I sank into the deep sleep that follows a first mountain day.

Though it seems they sang all night, the hospice was silent when we rose at four, and appeared deserted. Only the woman of the house was up, raking the embers of the fire to heat our coffee. Never were we failed by innkeeper, muleteer, or pathfinder. Once made, an assignation was kept. In this traditionally unpunctual country one could tell a muleteer to come back in so many days at noon, and confidently await his return. As we drank our coffee, Don Miguel joined us. He too had been up all night, though it was inconceivable that he should have been singing. With inward face, immobile, no doubt drunk, he had sat in the roaring room. I wondered what mechanics and muleteers thought of this presence on their mountain passes. We left him swaying at the door, yet without loss of dignity. After the kitchen, dense with the stale fumes of wine and brandy, the cold air made us shiver. Two stars still shone. Like black paper shapes pasted against the paling sky, the mountains though clear were not solid.

A brief valley, but remote and little visited, led us that morning to the Cresta d'Amitjes, the Ridge of the Friends. Though goats might do so, cattle and sheep could not reach the valley pastures, for the small lake which bars access to the valley is only turned by a scramble over polished boulders. They looked like the skulls of mammoths in the half-light. It always seizes disturbingly on things whitish: waterfalls glowed, water-scoured rocks gleamed like mirrors, and we noticed everywhere the scarce white alpine rose. By contrast, in this moment of white and grey, the pink alpine rose, drifts of shuttered gentians, a whole range of colour, did not exist. Through a defile of shadows we came to a large ruminating water, the lake of Gerbei. Without promontory or foreshore, it described a dark circle under the surrounding cliffs, as though a crater had been filled with ink. Now with the dawn 'rise' its forbidding surface was ringed again and again by the enormous fish that lived there, Don Miguel's trout, *grandes como perros*.

In a first thin sunlight we emerged above the lake to see our ridge gleaming in the sky beyond. With the clearness of early morning it seemed close and every detail of rock and snow engraved with finicky precision. We made easily towards it past a series of little lakes harboured between terraces of turf and rock. Climbing the slopes, we met each lake at eye level; to look back later on a succession of stepped waters, as elaborately artificial in their effect, and as pleasing, as the pools and basins of some great garden. There was nothing here to remind us of Lake Gerbei. These lakes offered intimacies, bays and isthmuses;

we could see the sunlight probing the sandy bottom and boulders lying there like huge whelks. Each patch of sky-reflecting blue had its contorted pine trees, never more than one or two, jutting over the water. Sometimes a pine grew from precarious foothold on a small rock-island. The detail was precise, the scale miniature, yet the setting immense. The scene recalled those Japanese prints in which one shapely tree and an improbable island, precisely delineated, are seen in surprising relation to snows and precipices. The water was stinging cold.

This effect of Japanese waterworks set among turf and flowers, of an upward progress from pool to waiting pool, is not unusual in the Spanish Pyrenees between the trough of the lower valley and the bare slopes above. But the twisted individual pine, the sense of intimacy, was soon left behind. Drifting screes succeeded and then drifts of snow. The final lake below the mountain *cirque* carried a floating sorbet, a mass of rotten snow. The water, a dark rim, was only visible round the melting edge. This was the spare valley-head. Above us, the Amitjes, a fine serrated ridge, had lost nothing in the approach. As we toiled up, a pair of wall-creepers, solitary birds, showed their wing coverts in startling crimson flashes. The ridge proved a disappointment for the ground on the south fell easily away. All the mountaineering interest it offered was a rock tower and snow-cornices, poised as though about to break, like a wave by Hokusai, over the small Japan now far below. Yet no day could have better returned us to these mountains, and no approach have so well expressed their character. Don Miguel had made his choice with care.

One other excursion in this time of initiation is worth recall, the three days that took us to the Gran Pic de Colomés. With loaded mule we set off from Salardu up the Rio Aiguamoch. Here was contrast to the region of Lake Gerbei. In form the valley resembled those of the French Pyrenees: a stretch of gentle inclination, a place where a stream might meander or lap over pebbles, a place suited to haymaking or the pasturing of cattle, would end abruptly in a mountain face hung with toppling boulders, leaning pines, and the white threads of cascades; here a giddy track zig-zagging to the crest would reveal another *jasse* or pastoral interlude, and beyond it a further mountain barrier. By contrasts and giant steps, the valley progressed to the last little lakes and the encircling snowpeaks at their head.

We did not at once leave village life behind. For an hour or more there were toy meadows bounded by dry-stone walls, and a stream edged with walnut and almond trees. Women in waisted black dresses raked hay into mounds, and men lowered their scythes as we passed. They were attacking swathes of flowers, for the meadows were not green but full of narcissi, and yellow and purple orchids. The scent of cut hay and flowers drifted across our track to mix with the not-unpleasant smell of mule droppings. Where the first mountain-step barred the valley, we looked back. The figures in the fields had diminished, but still moved with purpose. Distance had made them archetypes: they were the black-clothed women, the scything men, of all mountain valleys, the human dots seen always from far above, whether in the Pyrenees or the Alps, the outposts of organized society from which one is parting or to which one reluctantly returns.

Above, we entered the first smooth *jasse*, where the wizened cattle would come up to graze later in the summer. Here at a height between the meadow flowers and the alpine species, it was all feathery grasses, their seeding heads white in the sun and the seeds clinging to our stockings like powder snow. On an easy glinting bed the stream curved without sound. Only fritillaries and swallowtails were busy. The tranquil meadowiness gained half its point from the surrounding mountain slopes, the tumbling cascades, and the impending disorder of grey rock, pine, and cistus. To one side, where the mountain met the *jasse*, stood a dilapidated log-cabin. Our map marked the 'Bains de Tredos'. Forcing a door we found, in a reek of sulphur, bathing-rooms long-deserted, and the fragment of a linen towel worked in red gothic script with a coronet and the initials A.B. We pondered what aristocratic fancy, what hope of health or gain, could have established this remote Vichy, and who had bathed, and how long ago, in these sulphur springs. Angèle de Benasque? Or was she christened Astrée, Amélie, Ariane, Aréthuse, Aspasie? We imagined an orderly procession winding up the steep passage to the *jasse*. We followed in its wake to the sound of cool Castilian, the jingle of harness, and the smell of a rich Havana. In a wideawake hat and green corduroy suit, the Count, growing heavy, rode a powerful mule. Half-hidden in a gauzy veil, the Countess, nursing a complexion pallid as snow, rocked gently on her side-saddle as though riding a long sea-swell. Hers was an obscure complaint.

The tight-waisted gentleman behind her, his moustaches and beard clipped and trained like topiary, was the finest billiards player in court circles, and long her lover. The priest on a donkey clasped a basket. Within reposed the Host, discreetly covered with a napkin, for this was Sunday morning. Curved panniers fitted snugly over the flanks of sumpter mules (Pommery, Seltzer water, Liebig's Essence, a shoulder of mutton, a vial of laudanum, and apricots from the walled garden in Lower Aragon). The footmen, very properly on foot, perspired. Among the nodding grasses they set out chairs and plaid rugs from Scotland, put up the elaborate tents, and unpacked the white linen bathing-towels. A servant carried these, coronet uppermost, across to the cabin, its logs still new and raw, and deposited them dubiously on stone slabs beside the smelly sulphur pools . . .

Our mule was cooling its hooves in the stream, and we sat outside the Baths, speculating in the noonday pause on the loves and ailments of the Countess of Benasque (and drinking weak brandy and cold water to discourage the flies), when a man came quickly down the *jasse*, his stride cleaving the grasses. Though everything about him was purposefully native, we obscurely divined the approach of a countryman. This, the only Englishman I have met in the Spanish Pyrenees, was accoutred in a fashion that the Countess might almost have recognized. He was Belloc's Pyrenean Traveller. Dressed and provisioned to the rude prescription laid down half a century earlier by the giant walker, he wore a beret and *alpagates*, and he carried in his hand a staff and across his shoulder, for his casual bivouacs, a blanket. His haversack contained nothing but the routine *botta* of red wine, bread, and garlic sausage. Like Belloc, he travelled light, at a pace, and alone. We envied him his austerity and the spirit which made no concession to the changes of fifty years. He must have found contemptible our wickered demijohns and the sissy gear piled high on the tail-whisking mule; he refused with surprise our brandy and water. Such meetings are difficult.

He was our last human being. The Rio Aiguamoch was shrinking. Even the summer cattle rarely penetrated to the *jasse* beyond the next mountain step. Soon the Gran Pic de Colomés was in view, with its lanky arms embracing a snow-bowl and a scatter of high lakes. A final slope that taxed the mule brought us to our camp at evening, a mossy promontory, crowned with pines, 200 feet above a lake. In the course of a leisurely day we had passed from the narrow streets of the village, the black figures and the scythes, the deserted baths and the last traveller, to a landscape owing nothing to men. Beautifully exemplified, it had been the familiar grateful progression from society to silence, from complexity to the ivory towers of the mountains.

We lit an enormous fire to keep off the mosquitoes. Like the flies at noon, they presaged thunder. A few drops fell before we slept. 'A vile night', my diary reads, but I remember dozing off with the fire-shadows darting among the pine branches overhead. I suppose the mosquitoes attacked as the blaze died down. Next morning under a spitting sky we started for the Gran Pic de Colomés. Our lake was indigo and raked by scudding gusts. The day promised nothing. After an overcast night the snow was unfrozen, and we struggled knee-deep across the white bowl below the peak. A couloir and an icy slab took us to the east ridge. It had character. Between precipitous slopes an aery comb of granite led for half a mile towards the peak and then was lost in the imposing flanks of the final buttress. Never difficult, yet inducing care, it would have seemed a delightful passage but for the weather. We had held on our way thus far only by the familiar device of saying, 'Hopeless . . . the weather's worsening . . . we'll go just to the next lake . . . the next snow shoulder . . . the rock slab.' Now that subterfuge had brought us to the real climb, clouds were sagging into the valleys below and streamers swirled across the ridge, intermittently hiding the peak. We seriously paused. But retreat would now have been too disheartening; as it proved we took the right decision.

Though the wind jostled us on the rock, by the time the peak loomed above there were blue rents in the sky and the clouds were breaking. The change brought elation. Instead of climbing the mountain by an easy route from the south shoulder, we decided to attempt the east face. For sixty feet the issue was in doubt, but kindly ledge and fissure took us to easier rock. In half an hour we were on the summit, and perhaps had made a new route. The Gran Pic de Colomés is a noble mountain, and its views were worthy. As the clouds dispersed, R. and I saw the peaks we knew—Aneto, Beciberri, Fourcanade, Aiguilles de Travesany—and between them indications of folds and troughs, the high valleys where we had camped in the previous year. South-east we scanned through glasses two smooth grey teeth, and I took my second view of the Encantados.

The unexpectedness of success and the gift, now certainly ours, of a cloudless return sent us lilting past cornices along the crest to the subsidiary peak of the Petit Colomés. From there descent was not wholly easy. A scramble down rock ended in a precipitous gully. The snow was dangerous. Almost at a touch, a deep layer would peel off with a rustling sound and leave a track like a long tear stain. The edges of the gully were no better, for the snow lay on ice. But we eased ourselves on the rope to gentler ground. There was nothing more. With the sun on our backs, we walked across thinning snowslopes and past white lakes to the first pines, and so down to our mossy promontory and the demijohns. The sunset, making amends for dawn, was still and honeyed. We watched the night creep towards us, slowly filling the valleys eastward and rising like a dark liquid until it lapped about the camp. We lit another huge fire and went deeply to sleep with the smell of burning fir-cones.

*   *   *

Reality is unlikely to do much for places or persons that have led a privileged life in one's imagination. We might with reason have turned tail. But the Encantados were close and their time had now come. We drove one evening down the Noguera Pallaresa and up the dusty road to Espot by a succession of hairpin bends. We found a village that sat astride a stream, a solid romanesque spire, dirt in cobbled lanes, and the whisky that Don Miguel had predicted. The whisky was for fishermen who frequented the inn, their eyes bulging at the prospect of unctuous trout. To them we also owed well-sprung beds.

Next morning we rose late thinking only to explore the setting of the Encantados and prospect a route. A rough track ended, past the last cultivated fields, at the lip of a green entrenched valley. Only a mile off, we stared at our mountains. I could not judge them in climbing terms or assess their comparative difficulty. For me, by this time, there were no other peaks. After a two years' approach, they seemed superb and hardly to be surmounted. Transformed, as love always transforms its object, they had no deficiencies or faults. I have never seen the Encantados as they are.

They held our gaze as we walked towards them through a profusion of trees, the bowers of birds. I had not known such comfortable trees or so many birds could exist on these southern slopes. Serins, bullfinches, crested tits, even the mistrusting jay, were undisturbed by our passage. There was a constant rustling of wings in the branches. As we approached the lake of San Mauricio and the saint's shrine, built like a martin's nest below an overhanging rock, the Encantados grew in the sky. Deep clefts separated them from the peaks on either side and they rose isolated over the trees and the lake. Though they seemed so, these mountains were not big even by Pyrenean standards. The higher of the twin peaks was little over 9,000 feet. But the northern summit, some thirty feet lower, was the only serious mountain in the Pyrenees offering no easy route. Even the gash which separated it from the south summit was abrupt. On the saddle between, the Enforcadura, stood the isolated stone pinnacles to which the Encantados owe their name. Two shepherds trying to scale the peaks on a Sunday morning heard the sound of bells from the solid spire in Espot, and did not descend to mass. We were grateful that they had been summarily turned to stone. By so baptizing the Encantados they had brought us there.

Since I had seen, and sadly seen, from Menjou's supper table, the grey north peak falling its unconcerned length to the lake of San Mauricio, a year in England had only increased the aura of the Encantados and added little to our knowledge. In the seventh of Beraldi's authoritative and unreadable volumes on the history of the Pyrenees, we had learnt of the first ascent of the north summit in 1902. It pleased us that Colonel Brulle, the moving spirit, was a dandy, climbing 'tiré à quatre épingles, la guerre en dentelles', while his companion, Count D'Astorg, personified 'le mépris de la vulgarisation, du suissisme, du clubalpinisme et des yahous': an impressive but contemptuous couple. No less impressive was the description of their French guide surmounting the crux in stockinged feet, and the Colonel's laconic comment on return, 'long, pénible, difficile, dangereux'. In the *Revue Alpine* we had also read of the first ascent of its north face in 1926, the elegant route which had long held our thoughts.

During a winter's absence I had imagined the Encantados gathering snow like virtue and the splendour I could not share. Their white shoulders and polished slopes had recurred in dreams. Now lying in the shade I looked at them and was filled with content. The scene was such as Patinir might have painted: dramatic rock and hirsute mountain blending with humanized elements (the mule track, the flourishing glade, the unruffled water) to create a work of art. It was indeed an enchanted valley and these were enchanted peaks. The north face engaged our attention. Though no doubt less sheer than we imagined, it fell abruptly for over 2,500 feet to the lake and all these trees and birds. Isolated conifers attempted a brief ascent and hung over the valley from fissures in the rock. In such a situation firs and pines, trees that the twentieth century much despises, came wonderfully into their own. There is a reason for valley trees: one may guess or know why they were planted. Such solitary conifers, fiercely rooted, were a law to themselves, individual and uncompromising.

As we left the friendly birds and walked up the slopes to the first rock spurs, we acknowledged no intention of climbing.We could still touch the mountain ruminatively and walk along its base with appraising eye. After all, it was mid-morning: we had only a single rope and a meagre lunch in our rucksack.We seemed sane.When a likely route tempted up the cliffs, we thought in terms of exploration, and an hour later retreated in good humour from an over-hang. But the sun was shining on the lake and birds encouraged from the trees. The more curious had ventured up the slope and were watching on boulders. Air, cool but something less than a breeze, drifted through the valley. Not far off a chimney like a staircase led upward; we began almost casually to climb. The rock was delightfully warm, the footholds always present. So we emerged insensibly on the steep grey slabs that clad, like armoured plates, the lower half of the face. I have no idea why we persisted. In doing so, we courted failure. Perhaps we had already developed with the mountain one of those relationships in which no proof of intimacy satisfies, in which one jealous claim succeeds another. Possibly we tackled the Encantados by the hardest route, six hours too late, to convince ourselves of a union with the mountain closer than we had a right to expect.

The sun which had been friendly in the valley began to reflect scorchingly off the slabs. The holds became few and the exposure constant. When we found an iron peg it brought no reassurance, since it seemed that only a madman could have placed a peg in so senseless a position. Hours passed and the sun moved off the face. The lake of San Mauricio shrunk, and if the birds cared to look they saw us diminished to beetles. Everything shrunk but the slabs. No doubt we exaggerated the difficulties, and we grew desperately tired. But, strangely, we never doubted of success. Repeatedly when the rock might have halted us a way was revealed. Sometimes from a crux the mountain almost shamelessly beckoned us up.

A few hundred feet below the summit, the slabs mercifully disintegrated. A curious flute-like formation followed. We climbed a gigantic organ-loft, now clinging to the pipes, now escaping into capacious funnels. Progress was easier and the moment came when there seemed to be more sky, a sudden increase of light that filled not only our eyes but our bodies. We were nearing the top. Stepping out, we could have sung. For this moment we had looked, approaching and retreating, two years.

Though the mountain had waited, the day had not. The

sun was already off the distant white dome of the Colomés and the ranged peaks westward. We acknowledged—it had long been evident—that we should sleep with the Encantados. Yet the north peak was not the place. After a rest we started down to the Enforcadura. This is the normal route to and from the summit, but not altogether easy; the sole account we had read spoke of delicate moves and vertical chimneys. The descent proved intoxicating. Elation was our support and found unerringly each foothold in the failing light. The mountain had accepted us and we could make no mistake. A sixty-foot *rappel* took us down the last awkward bit. I can still trap the profound sense of happiness which I knew swinging in the gathering darkness above the stone Shepherds.

Beside them we ate what food remained, and put on pullovers and gloves. Groping by the light of a multitude of stars, we found two small thrones, and sitting belayed in our rope waited for the dawn six hours away. So immobilized, open to every influence, we caught the smell of pines rising from the valley and even the scent of flowers not far below. We heard the abysses breathing and the tinkle of a falling pebble. The Encantados began to talk. Though there was no wind, it grew cold and our position made it impossible to sleep. Dozing, one woke with a jerk, conscious of the darkness below. I do not regret the sleeplessness. Above us there was light. The immense east wall of the peak shone in the starlight, and the same light burnt on the outline of the Shepherds. It sparkled on distant ridges. The dome of the sky, for it was indeed a dome, echoed with it. No one who has lived only in valleys knows this echo and the brilliant air which sets it ringing. And the earth moved. One had always known this, and it had seemed to move on other nights, sleeping out in the desert or the mountains. But now on the Encantados the thing was confirmed beyond doubt. We had seen the sun go down, a solid red ball, and the stars appear tentatively and multiply; now as the earth turned, the constellations passed. Shivering, I watched them move across the sky. I understood the galaxies, not in the meaningless terms of light-years, but of something which linked me to them, which gave the Encantados their enchantment and even ourselves significance. Perched with a rope round my waist, I saw the machinery of time. I saw it, the whole grave procession, from midnight to morning.

Yet the fading of the stars was welcome. Merely human, I was glad as they went out, and searched eagerly for the first pale wash in the east. Stiff, with stilted movements, we left our thrones as soon as it was light. There was no elation now. We stumbled uncertainly down rocks and endless scree. It was a long return and the heat grew intense. As we approached the valley, we saw a movement among the trees that had nothing to do with birds. Looking more closely, we found the slopes busy with tiny soldiers. There was activity everywhere. Some were scavenging along the base of the rocks, some searching the bird bowers, some gesticulating towards the north face. A gun began to boom at intervals. On a knoll we distinguished a still black figure and knew who had alerted the frontier guards. They were enjoying the diversion of looking for bodies, and our return an hour later was an anticlimax. Parched, we sank at Don Miguel's feet and swallowed repeated draughts of water. A brandy bottle from his pocket circulated above our heads. It was finished when Menjou, flanked by two grinning brigands, stepped up in top boots. I noticed they were flecked with paint. The gun was still booming.

Later, when the soldiers had gone, the landscape re-settled, became itself again. Except that Don Miguel sat beside us, nothing here had changed in twenty-four hours. The birds were still frantic, the branches rustling as if in a breeze, and the reflection of the grey rock-face (no sign of climbing mannikins) lay easy on the lake. Westward, look-ing as it must usually look about noon, was the pass whence I had first appraised the Encantados. Among the pines below, in the pools of sun and shadow where I had once waded, surely the insect plankton still rose and fell. The far Pic de Colomés was stately as ever, and other mountains that had played a part in our prologue were recognizably themselves. Only we three had lost or gained. 'So you have climbed it,' Don Miguel said, 'and I, too, in a way.' He looked exhausted enough to have done so. 'It was a good route, though had you kept further to the right, straight up (I once told you), the slabs would have been less difficult.... Yet what, I wonder, brought you here from the Gave de Pau, and by so devious a way. Surely it was not I.' We had no reasons and could give no logical answer. That the trees were filled with birds, that the waters of the lake flowed down the valley, was evident to all but the trees and the water. Perhaps the pines or the lake may have known precisely what we were about. 'No reasons?' he said with satisfaction. 'I too had no reasons . . . in spite of this.' And he touched his black-trousered leg. 'You can reason to me of nothing that is important, neither this moment on this knoll, nor the Encantados, nor the people I have loved. You can reason of business and things unworthy of proof.'

We walked slowly down the valley, for that day Don Miguel was very lame. The black suit, faintly exhaling dust and brandy, looked almost grey in the bright light. We were surprised when he turned aside at the shrine of San Mauricio. 'A moment,' he said. Perhaps he had gone to say a prayer for our safe return. We felt suddenly insecure waiting in the warm sun. It seemed our future he should be praying for. We had long wanted one thing and now had been given it. We were without a goal; so perhaps was he. As we glanced back, the Encantados looked like any other mountain.

NOTES ON THE SPANISH PYRENEES

From the Val d'Estos to the Noguera Pallaresa

1. The Pyrenees are not a single straight line running 250 miles from Hendaye to Cape Cerberus, but two shorter and parallel lines which at the centre of the range briefly overlap. They are there bridged by a grassy link, the Bonaigüe pass at the head of the Val d'Aran. At this point some eight miles separate the two systems and their terminal peaks, the Pic de l'Homme on the north and the Pic de Sabouredo on the south. The curious position of the Val d'Aran, like a geographical fault, no doubt accounts for the fact that it is Spanish territory though lying to the north of the main watershed. Elsewhere the latter, with one or two exceptions, firmly divides Frenchmen and Spaniards.

   The Encantados, the Aneto, and other peaks mentioned in the text, lie at the eastern end of the Atlantic half of the range, and south of the bridge which links the Atlantic and Mediterranean Pyrenees.

2. Since 1953 certain valleys have felt the maleficent touch of progress. Hydro-electric works have come to San Mauricio, the lower Rio Malo, the upper Rio Aiguamoch, and the Rio Fougeras. Fortunately it seems that dams can be maintained without the presence of human beings. When the landscape has been scarred, the surgeons leave. Vegetation does its work. These valleys are not ruined. Others, and they are among the best, such as the Esera, the Estos, the Malibierne, the head-waters of the Noguera Ribagorzana, and the valley of Lake Gerbei, have so far been spared.

   A development more prejudicial to the area was the breaching of the Viella tunnel which in 1955 took a road across the seventy-five roadless miles that previously separated the passes of the Portalet and the Bonaigüe. It opened the heart of the range. But the damage is less than might be supposed. There are no hotels and the motor-cars hurry through.

3. There are now (1961) the following huts:

Rencluse (for the Aneto massif). 6 hours from Benasque. Key at the Fonda del Sayo, Benasque.

Estos (for the Posets, Pic d'Oo, etc). $4\frac{1}{2}$ hours from Benasque. Key at the Fonda del Sayo, Benasque.

José Maria Blanc (for the Monastero, Peguera, etc). $3\frac{1}{2}$ hours from Espot. Key at Hotel Saurat, Espot.

Joan Ventosa i Calvell (for Beciberri, Aiguilles de Travesany, etc). 3 hours from Caldas de Bohi. Key at village of Bohi.

With the exception of the Rencluse, these huts have neither blankets nor equipment and offer mere refuge.

4. Inns, with the exception of the Hotel Saurat at Espot and the establishment at Caldas de Bohi, are primitive. But there is welcome at the Fonda del Sayo at Benasque, and at the Hotel la Creu at Salardu. The Hospice de Viella and the Hospice de Nuestra Senhora de los Ares, at the headwaters respectively of the Noguera Ribagorzana and Noguera Pallaresa, date from the Middle Ages and offer a comfort appropriate to that period. Mules are to be had, with some delay, at all these places.

5. Usually one will camp at a valley head. Food is cheap and, with the exception of butter, easily bought in the bigger villages. Wine and brandy are even cheaper. In most villages someone speaks French. If not, one must hope that the local tongue is Spanish and not Catalan. Though the weather may be good by alpine standards, a tent is essential. For weather, flowers, and green in these southern places, not to speak of the quality of the snow, May and June are the best months, though early July will do.

6. The Mountains straddle the last of Catalonia and the first of Aragon. This is fortunate, since the frontier guards of these provinces have little friendship and no liaison.

By comparison with the Alps the climbing is modest. The

summits are relatively low and the glaciers few. On the other hand there are no detailed guidebooks (as exist for the French slopes of the Pyrenees), and no guides who climb. Apart from the mule tracks across the passes, there are no paths. A morning may be wasted in a wilderness of stones, a mountain forfeited by a scramble to a delusive col. Even the most obvious routes on the best rock have been little cleared by predecessors. New climbs are still to be made. The pleasure is in the wildness.

The quality of the rock varies. But there is a respectable granitic vein that runs from the Pic d'Oo towards the Encantados. Apart from climbs mentioned in the text, the Posets, the Maladetta, the Col Maudit, and the north ridge of the Peguera offer rewarding routes. The *Revue Alpine* for 1927 (vol. xxvii, no. 3) describes further climbs of a more acrobatic nature. They include the Profil de Monseigneur, Petite Aiguille de la Ratère, Aiguilles de Basiero, and Las Tres Pouys.

7. Belloc (*The Pyrenees*, 1900) remains the best introduction to the range, and Pierre Soubiron (*Les Pyrénées*, Librairie Soubiron, Toulouse, N.D.) the best general guide to the area. One may also read Charles Packe's *Guide to the Pyrenees* (1862); Henry Russell's *Souvenirs d'un Montagnard* (1878); and Harold Spender's *Through the High Pyrenees* (1898). Little written since will give comparable pleasure, though J. Soler's *La Vall d'Aran* (1906) and M. Gourdon's *Au Pays d'Aran* (1924) are useful. A good alpine flora includes most of the flowers, and the birds are covered by *A Field Guide to the Birds of Europe* (Collins 1954).

8. Maps:

F. Schrader: Pyrénées Centrales (6 sheets), 1/100,000; Instituto Geografico: (sheets 148–9, 180–1), 1/50,000; Centro Excursionista de Cataluña: Maladetta, and Caldas de Bohi (2 sheets), 1/25,000.

None of these maps is altogether reliable. Useful information as to local conditions is to be had, and readily, from the Centro Excursionista de Cataluña, Paradis 10, Barcelona.

INDEX